# single jewish female

## A MODERN GUIDE TO SEX AND DATING

# single jewish female

## A MODERN GUIDE TO SEX AND DATING

Leah Furman

A PERIGEE BOOK

A Perigee Book
Published by The Berkley Publishing Group
A division of Penguin Group (USA) Inc.
375 Hudson Street
New York, New York 10014

First Perigee paperback edition: September 2004

ISBN: 0-399-53019-3

Visit our website at
www.penguin.com

Library of Congress Cataloging-in-Publication Data

Furman, Leah.
    Single Jewish female / Leah Furman.—1st Perigee pbk. ed.
        p. cm.
    "A Perigee book."
    ISBN 0-399-53019-3
    1. Jewish women.  2. Single women.  3. Dating (Social customs)
4. Man-woman relationships.  I. Title.

HQ1172.F87 2004
646.7'7'082—dc22                                        2004048352

Printed in the United States of America

10   9   8   7   6   5   4   3   2   1

# contents

# acknowledgments

I couldn't have written this book without the many Jewish women, and men, who responded to my questions, both in person and over the Internet. Thank you all for having so much patience in the face of my sometimes intrusive interrogation. It was all done in the name of research. I had to know: What does being Jewish have to do with sex and dating? Thank you for providing me with so many different perspectives and helping me open my mind and look at every side of this issue.

I also have to thank my agent, Jane Dystel, who warmed to this topic from the start and whose enthusiasm enabled this book's publication. Christel Winkler and Sheila Curry Oakes, my editors at Perigee Books, deserve a great deal of credit for their vision, feedback, and encouragement.

My family, as always, was a tremendous source of support. My friends as well . . . I would mention all of you by name, but you know who you are and you know that I love you and thank you!

Finally, thanks to the guys I've dated during my years as an SJF. . . . And thanks to the ones who continue to date me, knowing their story may wind up in a book.

# introduction

## What's So Funny?

When I first had the idea for this book, I envisioned it as an irreverent and humorous look at what it means to be Jewish, single, and female. Initially, Judaism seemed like a gold mine of comedic opportunity. I planned to cover all the Jewish mating rituals, jokes, and stereotypes and maybe even come up with a few of my own in the process. It would be hysterical. Or so I thought. Then, I started doing the research.

In talking to Jewish women about their love lives, I was surprised at how little I actually found to laugh about. Although a few did treat the topic lightly, happy to put that aspect of their identity and self-concept on the back burner, most were quite serious about the heritage and what it means to them. There were stories of interfaith dating, heartbreak, personal struggle, and spiritual transformation. Suddenly, being Jewish didn't seem all that funny.

Needless to say, I was not thrilled about any of this. I was going for witty, clever, and caustic. Something that would fly in the face of tradition and maybe even get me barred from a few seder tables. I was not going for anything heavy, serious, or overly compassionate. But here I was, talking to Jewish women, reading about Judaism, and finding meaning and spirituality for the first time in my life. What would this mean for the book, I wondered. Would I still be able to keep it light and breezy?

I mean, I had absolutely no intention of changing my point of view when this all began. Like I said, the book was going to be funny, *not*—I repeat *not*—eye opening, insightful, or profound. After all, I'd had plenty of opportunities to embrace Judaism through the years. And never once did I succumb. Why did this have to happen now?

Looking back, I suppose it all makes sense in retrospect. My life started out Godlessly enough, back in the Soviet Union: Atheism was the national religion, Lenin and Stalin our gods. In school, faith was treated like a big joke. I was only eight when we left, but I got the message. There was no God.

Despite having no knowledge of the Torah, however, I was still acutely aware of my Jewish identity. Ever since the age of four, my parents and grandparents were warning me: "Don't tell anyone where your grandmother lives." My grandmother had emigrated to Israel when I was still a baby. To this day, I attribute every nursery school and kindergarten teacher's dislike of me to rabid anti-Semitism.

I quickly realized why we had left Ukraine during our journey to the States. While we were staying in Italy, waiting for the arrangements for our arrival in the United States to be finalized, my father was initiated into Orthodox Judaism by a group of rabbis who made it their mission to educate Soviet Jews. Overnight, we went from being strict secularists to God-fearing, *Shema*-reciting, ham-eschewing super-Jews.

When we got to the United States, I quickly assimilated to the ways of American Jews. For a few years, I even went to Jewish day schools. My first two years were at the Orthodox Hillel Torah. Then I lobbied my parents and won a transfer to the conservative Solomon Schechter school. Finally, I had a Bat Mitzvah and began going to public school. I lived in a safe, sheltered, predominantly Jewish suburb. As far as I was concerned, the whole world was Jewish and anti-Semitism was just something that happened in the "wrong" areas.

Having come of age around so many Jews, I rarely thought about what I had in common with other Jewish women. Mostly, I spent my time concentrating on all the things that made me different. As it turns out, I was not alone. Many of the women I spoke to, who grew up surrounded by Jews, were no longer affiliated with the Jewish culture either. For many of us, it is not until we start moving into our thirties that we begin to feel a nostalgia for our past and a yearning for Jewish community.

Meanwhile, here I was, thinking I was so different, so enlightened, so beyond the pull of religion, when all this time I'd been on the very same path as hundreds of thousands of Jewish women before me. Nowadays, I'm through trying to be different. Just trying to be myself is a challenge all its own. Especially when I consider the role Judaism plays in who I am and who I hope to be.

As I was writing this book, I found that a lot of people were curious about what makes Jewish women special. The most popular question I heard was: "Why do Jewish women need their own dating book? How are Jewish women different?"

The truth is, we're not different. However, we do have something special in common. Due to our similar backgrounds, upbringings, experiences, and traditions, we share a certain set of expectations for how our lives will play out. These are the ties that bind and divide us. Some of us have followed the chosen path from day one, content to date Jewish men and think of raising Jewish children, others have wandered and found their way back, and still others have flown the coop for good. But no matter how our personal experiences and perspectives may divide us, our parents will always be Jewish, our first memories will always be Jewish, and we'll never laugh at a Jewish joke unless it is delivered by a fellow Jew.

As single Jewish females looking for love, sex, fun, marriage, or any combination of the above, we have many issues and concerns in common. It stands to reason that by opening up and telling our stories like a group of girlfriends, we could help one another get through tough times; prepare for the future; and come to understand, accept, and celebrate those aspects of our culture that make our paths through life unique.

Although I began with the intention of making this book an amusing, laugh-inducing read, I ended up with something completely different. *Single Jewish Female: A Modern Guide to Sex and Dating* is half self-help and half how-to. You'll read about Jewish identity and Judaism's take on such topics as dating etiquette, self-preservation, and sexual practices as well as how to meet Jewish men and how to navigate relationships with Jews and non-Jews alike. This is not to say that there won't be any humor, just that comedy is not the focus of this book. Figuring out what Judaism has to do with sex and dating, infusing your personal life with spirituality and meaning, and becoming the strong, confident Single Jewish Female (SJF) you always wanted to be . . . that's what this book is all about.

# chapter one

## What's God Got to Do with It?

*I stopped going to temple when I was about fourteen. I just told my mom what I still believe to this day, that I am against organized religion because it breeds hatred. (She loved that.) When I was sixteen, she told me that if I didn't go to temple on the holidays then I had to go to school; I could no longer spend the holidays sleeping in. I guess my mom thought she'd win with the whole "what sixteen-year-old would pass up an opportunity to miss school" angle. But, since my mom and dad went to temple together, in one car, I saw this as a perfect opportunity to drive my mom's car to school . . . and seized it. In the end, it was a perfect arrangement for me.*

*After age fourteen, I think I went to temple three times: my grandfather's funeral, my younger cousin's Bat Mitzvah, and my other cousin's wedding. I hated all of those experiences. Each time I'd step foot in a synagogue, I'd instantly regress to a twelve-year-old mind-set. This year, I made my fourth visit. I went to temple with my dad's side of the family, in Indianapolis, during Rosh Hashanah. I had just moved to Chicago and wanted to see my family very badly. So when they invited me in for the holiday, I went. Out of respect, I attended very long services with them. I guess a part of me thought I might go and have some renewed respect or awe for my heritage . . . but I was just really bored and frozen by their way too powerful AC.*

—Randi, twenty-six, Chicago

We Jew gals are a motley crew. Some of us make Judaism the focal point of our identities. We display our Jewish pride and traditional values by never missing a chance to go to temple, hosting Shabbat dinners for our Jewish friends, and throwing our unequivocal support behind Israel. Others, like Randi, relegate Judaism to the very periphery of our self-concepts. We show our universalist sentiments and progressive beliefs by eating bacon cheeseburgers on Yom Kippur, dating non-Jews on Friday nights, and even going so far as to support Palestinian statehood initiatives.

However, no matter what we do (short of accepting Jesus Christ as our personal savior and breaking our poor mothers' hearts), we'll always think of ourselves as Jewish. And not just because last names like Cohen, Bernstein, and Schwartz make it impossible for us to forget; not just because small towns in the Bible Belt make us feel uneasy; and not just because many of our parents make it their business to constantly remind us.

No, we think of ourselves as Jewish because Judaism is more than a religion. To be Jewish, we need never darken the doorstep of a synagogue, observe any specific holidays, or even believe in God for that matter. We need only be born to a Jewish mother and we're in. That's right, just as Jewish as any Hasid in a black fedora and beard. Thanks, Mom.

The fact that most of us call ourselves agnostic shows that Judaism as a faith is the dominion of the Orthodox, who account for less than 10 percent of all Jews. And while theirs is a vocal and powerful minority, the truth is that for the rest of us, Judaism is a culture. A legacy. An inherent distinction that makes us different in the eyes of billions.

Of the five billion people living on the face of the planet, only about thirteen million are Jews. Do the math and that's 0.0026 percent. For every ten thousand people, only twenty-six or so are Jewish. Yes, we're way outnumbered. Always have been. Always will be. No wonder our parents, maybe even a few of us, exhibit such extreme reactions upon learning that a recent homicide or car crash struck down a fellow Jew. Our numbers are low enough as it is.

If you're wondering what any of this has to do with your love life, look no farther. In this chapter, you'll learn why some women stick to dating Jews while others decide to expand their horizons. You'll also read about the reasons some of us are so involved in Judaism while others seem like they couldn't care less. You'll read about how:

- Your affiliation with Jewish identity can shift over time.

- Embracing your particular style of Judaism helps allay the confusion presented by different points of view.

- The Jewish community picks up where religion leaves off.

- Jewish guilt and fear may affect your dating decisions.

- The prospect of family and children can either lead us to or away from the faith.

## JEWISH AS WE WANNA BE: KNOWING OURSELVES

*I was not raised religious. But at twelve, I "returned" because of my identity politics. I was very influenced by my Holocaust-survivor grandmother and felt my Jewishness was extremely important. I wanted to practice my Judaism in the most authentic way possible—Orthodoxy.*

*I found myself trapped in a neurotic, stifling world that negated my personal identity and creativity. So when I was twenty-four, I became completely secular and have been much, much happier and able to accept myself as a person who is imperfect. If I am not able to practice thousands of rules of conduct and ritual for every moment of my life, it doesn't mean that God and I cannot or should not love me.*

*—Mindy, twenty-six, Santa Fe*

When we're dating and getting to know a variety of new people, we need to know who we are first. How else can we possibly do what every self-help guru in the field keeps telling us . . . just be ourselves? The funny thing about Judaism is that it has the potential to make self-awareness something of a challenge.

Judaism is complex enough in and of itself. If the faith was simply a religion, maybe life would be easier. Of course, being Jewish has never been easy. To complicate matters, an entire country of secular Jews, Israel, has turned being Jewish into a nationality. The Reform movement, meanwhile, has transformed the Jewish faith into community and culture. And, most recently, thanks to *Seinfeld* and half the characters of *Friends* (Monica and Ross Gellar and Rachel Green), Judaism has become as popular with gentiles as bagels and whitefish salad. So, whether or not you believe that Jews are God's Chosen People is really besides the point. You can still be as Jewish as you want to be.

Or not. We always have a choice: Deny our heritage or accept it. Ignore it or embrace it. Most of us end up doing both at various stages of our lives. Rejecting our roots works wonders when we're going through our rebellious phases. We get a chance to break from our parents, our community, and our heritage to establish our own entirely unique identity. Eventually, however, we grow comfortable enough with our individuality to allow tradition and the sense of peace that comes with it back into our lives.

In the end, we may not count ourselves among the Torah-thumping true believers, but we are continually numbered among the Jews. The option to explore our culture and develop a measure of ethnic pride is always open to us. And it is an option many of us embrace when we're feeling lost and need something concrete to guide us and give our lives structure.

Think back on your own life and answer these questions:

- When did you feel most Jewish?

- When did Judaism have no bearing on your self-concept whatsoever?

- When did you look at your fellow Jews and say, "What? These are my people? No, I don't think so."

Now, use the following time line to plot the stages of your Jewish identity. Consider the baseline itself as neutral, a time when your Judaism was a nonissue. As you chart your progress, see if you can link your sense of Jewish identity to particular events and transitions in your life.

MOST IDENTIFIED

Birth ———————————————————————————— Now

LEAST IDENTIFIED

When you've finished the exercise, connect the dots. Is there a zigzag pattern or have you always felt exactly the same about your unique birthright? Chances are you've probably had your fair share of mixed emotions. What triggered your personal transformations? Did your peers, partners, or parents have anything to do with it? Take some time to think about how external events affected your state of mind and identity.

*I was never too big on the whole Jewish thing growing up. I grew up in a very WASP-y neighborhood where being a Jew wasn't nearly as cool as it was at the high schools and junior highs of many of my current co-workers. Fitting in meant owning a horse, not a Jeep Cherokee. I even pledged a non-Jewish sorority at Vassar.*

*I didn't get in touch with my Jewish roots until I took a Judaism course in my sophomore year. I don't know if it was the charismatic professor, the subject matter, or the fact that my life was pretty chaotic at the time, but for the next three years, I was completely hooked on religion. In retrospect, I think I used Judaism to help me cope with some personal problems I was having and feeling out of control in my life, because right now, I'm really into my work and engaged to a non-Jew. I don't have much time to devote to religion.*

—Sara, thirty-five, Boston

No matter how old you are, the changes never end. Our relationship to Judaism is likely to take as many hairpin turns and corkscrew twists in the future as it has in the past. Even those of us who insist that religion is a "crutch" or "the opiate of the masses" may one day realize that a crutch or an opiate is just what the Jewish doctor ordered when we're limping in pain.

"I may not have had a hard life, but I have been through a lot psychologically," says twenty-three-year-old SJF Renata. "I often think that if I become more in touch with God than I have been in the past, things will get better. Maybe if I become a 'better Jew,' I will not experience such sorrow. Maybe if I go to synangogue —at least for Yom Kippur—my life will be happier."

Whether or not we ever open our hearts to the religious dimension of Judaism, one thing is certain: Our ideas about the Jewish tradition, message, and community will not remain static. If we hope to forge meaningful relationships with Jewish men, or non-Jewish ones for that matter, we have to be honest with ourselves about the effect Judaism has on our self-concepts and worldviews. We must think through the various implications that Judaism has on our lives.

If we're unaffiliated Jews, who never go to temple but feel a strong emotional connection to the tradition of our ancestors, we must acknowledge and embrace this reality. If we've grown up surrounded by Jews and wish to remain in close quarters with our community—despite our lack of religious beliefs—we need not feel ashamed because we're not interested in stepping outside our comfort zones. There is no right or wrong way to be Jewish. We need to own our Jewishness . . . no matter what form it takes.

## A COMMON BOND: KNOWING OUR PARTNERS

*Now that I've actually experienced a long-term relationship, I realize that there are certain practical considerations that could lead one to want to date another Jew. Namely, the closer you are in background to the person you are dating, the easier time you will have understanding each other.*

*For instance, my boyfriend and I both have fathers who are engineers (i.e. distant) so we have an easier time understanding each other's issues. I think I would have broken up with him years ago rather than deal with his Israeli mother—if I didn't have an Israeli parent of my own. And the fact that we both went to Orthodox high schools means that there's a lot of mental warping that we have in common that would just seem like ordinary insanity to someone who didn't share that experience. I feel that our shared background as American Jews of partially Israeli parentage and Orthodox schooling makes it easier for us to accept each other.*

*—Elizabeth, twenty-six, St. Louis*

Once we've established a strong sense of identity, getting to know other people becomes considerably easier. We stop worrying about what we look, act, and sound like and start concentrating on the person standing in front of us. The questions come naturally: Where are they from? What are they like? What kind of values do they have? What do they think about this, that and the other?

Sometimes, you meet someone and you feel that immediate sense of recognition. You talk a bit more, and it turns out both of you grew up in predominantly Jewish suburbs, spent summers at similar sleep-away camps, and nearly botched your haftorah readings at your Bar and Bat Mitzvahs. Next thing you know, you're either (1) staring at each other with that "Omigod! We have so much in common!" look in your eye and thinking about *huppahs,* guest lists, and baby names or (2) running for the nearest exit and wondering how two people with exactly the same background could have wound up so different.

Case 1 marks the beginning of a beautiful friendship. Case 2 is the reason many of us SJFs often steer clear of our male counterparts. "I have a hard time meeting Jewish men," says Sharone, a twenty-six-year-old personal chef from Manhattan. "I am an unconventional Jewish girl. I do not fit the profile of the typical Jewish girl. I have been on soooo many bad dates with Jewish men."

Clearly, we're not going to get along with every Jew just because we come from the same stock. In fact, our different perceptions of the same experiences may divide us more than they bring us together. "What?! You didn't like Bar Mitzvah season?" you say, thinking that you could never in a million years see yourself with someone so antisocial. "How's that? You actually liked your high school?" you exclaim, thinking that anyone so mainstream could never fit in with your unconventional attitude. Usually, our disappointed expectations are the culprits. We naturally believe that anyone in his right mind would see the world as we do. When he doesn't, we chalk it up to fundamental differences.

Then again, when we do hit it off with a fellow member of the tribe, things are that much smoother, clearer, and, yes, funnier. Even perennial Jew-shunners like Randi from Chicago can't deny the bonding that can occur between two like-minded Jews. "I have never dated a Jewish boy," Randi says, "but one of my closest girlfriends is Jewish and before I met her . . . well, let's just say there is a lot to be said for hanging out with someone who is basically you. Things are easier. We get each other's jokes and sense of humor. Plus we can make fun of our moms for the same things."

Getting to a point of intimacy with another person is difficult enough without the nagging questions, doubts, and misper-
ceptions that can arise from two disparate backgrounds. We can
spend months just trying to unravel the cultural maze that con-
tributed to creating our partner's outlook, whereas sticking with
Jews allows us to relax and enjoy the comraderie that comes
with a collective subconscious and a "Jewish sensibility."

Even when we date outside our flock, we often look for
what's familiar, characteristics associated with our own culture:
Warmth, humor, and affection. "I just like the way Jewish guys
interact with their family," says Jessie, a twenty-three-year-old
SJF from Boston. "They can just be themselves, where I find that
a lot of Christain guys have to put on a happy face around their
families and they can't really 'be.' I haven't had too many Jewish
dating experiences, but my current boyfriend is very Jewish acting, he's very sensitive and emotional, which is what I like."

Being with another Jew cuts down on the getting-to-know-
you phase of the romance. A shared culture provides context clues
we can draw on to enrich our understanding and help us navigate
the path to mutual understanding, acceptance, and unconditional
support. "Judaism plays a large cultural role more than a religious
or spiritual one," says Mike, a thirty-one-year-old SJM from
Chicago. "On that level it is important to date Jews for me because there is some sort of 'understanding' that we have. Like being on the same page. The idea of us being a tribe is true on some
level. Maybe some gene that gives us all the ability to complain,
have bad stomachs, and eat lox. That said, having dated Jews and
non-Jews, I realize it's more like the extra layer of cake on an
eight-layer cheesecake. Always nice, but not necessary."

Since similar backgrounds are not a prerequisite to a good
relationship, and many SJFs don't even know what it feels like to
be in love with a fellow tribester, some of us sacrifice our desire

for a Jewish partner to the gods of love, passion, and companionship. To hear most Jewish women and men tell it, however, in an ideal world, we'd all have that extra layer of cake—a relationship with someone who not only comes from the same upbringing but who also shares our particular perception of the experience.

## THE JEWISH CONSPIRACY:
## KNOWING OUR FUTURE

*I am not an extremely religious Jew and, although I was raised in a very Jewish community, most of my friends were not very religious either. I can't read Hebrew, don't keep kosher, rarely go to temple, and celebrate only the very major Jewish holidays. Still, Judaism plays a huge part in my dating life. Growing up I dated only Jews because those were the people I was surrounded by and who I was attracted to. I went to a northeastern college with a huge Jewish population. I spent most of my social life with other Jews and dated accordingly. I always assumed I would marry someone Jewish because I was raised with such strong ties to the Jewish community. Ninety-eight percent of my friends are Jewish. There is just something comforting about being with people who understand your background, your family, the way you were raised. I have found there was always something missing in my friendships with non-Jews that I didn't want missing in a relationship.*

*—Andi, twenty-six, Miami*

"Life has taught us that love does not consist in gazing at each other," said Antoine de Saint-Exupéry, "but in looking outward together in the same direction." For many SJFs, that direction is defined by the Jewish community, the conglomerate of Jews who put aside personal differences and work together to promote and perpetuate the Jewish culture.

By raising money for Israel, going to synagogue, and patronizing Jewish cultural events at the Jewish Community Center (JCC), Jews bond to form a lifestyle and a thriving Jewish community. For many SJFs, the advantages of dating within the confines of these communities are multifold. For instance, consider the following.

## LIFE IS LIKE A BOWL OF CHERRIES

When you're dating someone from your community, you know what to expect. None of this Forrest Gump, "box of chocolates, you never know what you're going to get" business. For SJFs like Andi, life is unpredictable enough without taking a chance on your life partner.

## EVERYONE PITCHES IN TO HELP

No sooner do you graduate from college than the yenta machine shifts into high gear. Community members take the mitzvah of match making seriously. Within a month of graduation, I personally had four dates with nice Jewish boys set up by my parents, their friends, and co-workers.

Male or female, every Jew has an inner yenta dying to get out. Just last month, I was at a dinner party listening to one of the Jewish guests going on and on about his match-making prowess. "Jonathan and Ally just got engaged," he said. "That's my fourth mitzvah." When I asked what he meant, he proudly explained that three of the couples he'd fixed up have since gotten married.

*One of my Jewish co-workers started trying to set me up the moment she learned I had just broken up with my boyfriend. She was so helpful, always trying to set me up with her fiance's single friends. That's how I met my boyfriend. Many of his friends are now dating my girlfriends. It's really fun. We all go out together every weekend and have a great time.*

—*Abby, twenty-three, Los Angeles*

## SHARED VISION OF THE FUTURE

If an SJF is lucky enough to meet someone she likes from her community, the prospect of an uncertain future disappears all together. You'll follow in your parents footsteps and rest easy in the knowledge that come what may, you'll at least contribute to Jewish society.

The allure of a predictable future, however, is not for everyone—especially when that future is predicated on a less than stellar past. Despite our communities' best intentions, many SJFs and SJMs don't have the ultimate in coming-of-age experiences. Unlike their shiny, happy classmates, the disaffected Jewish youth often associate Jewish community with feelings of claustrophobia and dissatisfaction.

When we harbor negative emotions toward our formative experiences, they color our perceptions and turn all the benefits of dating within the Jewish community into drawbacks. Instead of feeling a sense of relief that our date is from the same background, we feel like all the mystery and fun have just been sucked out of getting acquainted. We know what we're going to get, all right: Exactly what we don't want. "Snobby, lazy, money-oriented Mama's boys" was how more than one SJF described Jewish guys.

The community's desire to see all of us perfectly matched also becomes more of a nuisance than a great way to meet new people. A fix-up or blind date is the kiss of death to be avoided at all costs. One SJM I spoke to recalled the following event: "I was cornered at synagogue by my mother and the mother of a girl. The first praying I'd ever done in the temple was for assistance from this onslaught. I even asked Jesus to help me. I remember taking a phone number. I remember the girl looking me up and down with thoughts of what color she might paint our second child's room." (Clearly, SJMs have developed some stereotypes for us as well. . . . )

Sharing a vision is still well and good—just as long as both parties agree on a future that bears no resemblance to the past. Quite a few of the women I interviewed made it clear that nothing could be less appealing than spending a lifetime feeling the way they did while in "captivity." To many of us, the following scenario, described to me by a staunchly unaffiliated SJF, is more nightmare than dream:

> There's a whole community of young Jewish adults in Orlando that started nursery school at the JCC, went through every summer in camp there, went off to the University of Florida and joined the Jewish sororities and fraternities, returned home each summer to work as counselors at JCC's day camp, and then moved back to Orlando after college. They all intermingle in young Jewish twentysomething social gatherings, marry each other, procreate, and put their own kids into the JCC's nursery school to perpetuate the cycle. This pattern, of course, happened long before I entered this world, and will continue to happen as far as I can see.

After thousands of years, Jewish community remains the centerpiece of Jewish culture. Whereas we were once bound to our roots by a hostile outside world, we are now free to move around at will. Still, the community exerts a powerful magnetic pull. I remember an incident at the University of Illinois, a school of some twenty thousand students, that perfectly illustrated the different perspectives of Jews. Two members of the Jewish sorority Sigma Delta Tau were discussing the university's dating pool.

"We don't have to restrict ourselves to these guys," the first sorority girl said, referring to the members of Zeta Beta Tau, Alpha Epsilon Pi, and Sigma Alpha Mu, the three Jewish fraternities on campus.

"Who else would we date?" said the second sorority girl.

"There's thousands of guys here," said the first.

The second girl looked skeptical and unconvinced, but said nothing.

Two completely different points of view. Both equally valid. Many of us stay put, happy in the safety and security of the only environment we've ever known, others experiment and return to the fold after years adrift, and still others find they are better suited to life on the outside and fly the coop for good. Chances are, you already know where you stand today. You're either in or you're out. The next section will discuss where you might decide to go in the future.

## BORN-AGAIN JEWS:
## GOING FROM CASUAL TO SERIOUS

*I wouldn't date boys who weren't Jewish all through high school. I recall having an argument with a friend of a friend. He was asking me out and I told him I wouldn't date non-Jews, but he kept insisting it was because he was black. When I got to college, I fell for a boy who was not only a non-Jew, but who had never met a Jew until he went to college!*

*We dated for three years, and it was pretty heavy. I used to think we could run away to another state and start out with*

## PANIC IN THE SHUL

Many SJFs make a conscious decision to partner with fellow Jews because we enjoy the sense of comfort and stability that comes with shared traditions, values and ideas of the future. Unfortunately, some of us are pressured and bullied into making what would otherwise be a well-reasoned and sensible choice by fear and propaganda. With so many solid, life-affirming reasons to marry Jewish, the last thing we need to worry about are the following emotionally charged arguments for doing the same:

- **The silent Holocaust:** This is the name some extremists give the high interfaith marriage rate for Jews in the United States. They contend that Hitler wins every time a Jew marries a gentile. Of course, long before Hitler ever came to power, progressive, free-thinking German Jews were intermarrying at a dizzying rate. Hitler put an end to all that. So remember the Holocaust, but forget Hitler when it comes to making your decisions. He wins when we allow him to dictate our behavior from the grave.

- **Survival of the species:** Jewish demographics are on the decline. Despite the high birth rate in Orthodox communities, our numbers are staying static. Many worry that pretty soon, Jews will die out all together. If we look at this argument within a historic framework, we'd realize that there has never been a time when Jews were not worried about dying out. And yet, 3,500 years later, we're still here.

- **Don't turn your back on your ancestors:** Are you willing to end 3,500 years of tradition with one choice? Break a chain that has been passed down from father to son, mother to daughter for countless generations? Such questions can only detract from the value we put on Judaism. If we take a serious look at Jewish culture and decide to do our part in furthering the line because it's what we want for ourselves and our children, so much the better. If, on the other hand, we find ourselves playing guessing games with the ghosts of our ancestors, wondering what on earth possessed them to stick with Judaism when we couldn't care less no matter how hard we try, restricting our dating to Jews would be an empty decision devoid of any personal meaning.

- **Your kids will be screwed up:** This one takes the cake. As if we didn't all know plenty of kids who were screwed up despite the fact that they were 100 percent Jewish. Just as children of mixed ethnic lineage are not necessarily tolerant and multicultural, neither are they inevitably lost souls who are clueless about their identity.

*no religion at all and no one would bother us. But it never felt realistic. There were definite cultural differences. When I met my husband, I knew the other relationship was just a college romance.*

—Marlene, forty-eight, Paramus, New Jersey

The passage of time brings significant changes for both men and women. Most of us undergo a gradual transformation between our early and late twenties (of course, the specific time frame varies from one individual to the next). We go from casual dating and open-ended relationships to searching for security and a life partner. This transition to a more serious frame of mind is rarely a smooth ride. In fact, a recent book by Alexandra Robbins and Abby Witner even termed this time the "quarter-life crisis."

If we were once most interested in the next party, shopping spree, or money-making opportunity, we are now soul searching, rediscovering the basics, and questioning who we are and what is truly important to us. What gives our life meaning? How do we find the strength and sense of purpose we need to carry on? Are we living our own lives or trying to live up to the expectations of others? What do we need to be happy? What kind of relationships do we want to negotiate with our friends, our families, and our significant others?

The incessant self-evaluation that goes on around this period can result in a variety of outcomes. The following are the four most common.

## WE RETURN TO JUDAISM

After we've sown our wild oats, we begin to take ourselves more seriously. Many who once rolled their eyes at the mere mention of "spirituality" begin to acknowledge that there may be something more to Judaism than empty ritual and shallow social customs. The 1990 Council of Jewish Federations Population Survey found that almost 22 percent of Jews are more Jewish now than they were growing up. If that statistic is any indication, many of us can no longer dismiss religion as easily as we did during our pleasure-seeking, fly-by-the-seat-of-our-pants days. We realize that even if religion does not define us it can in fact enhance us.

For some, faith in the Torah serves as the cornerstone of this transformation. When God is on our side, the future is no longer uncertain and we are no longer alone. While she's only twenty-four, Victoria is already a prime example of someone whose newfound love for God has given her a new lease on life and infused her existence with meaning, purpose and joy:

> I woke up when a friend told me that a family member of his had been near death after an accident. He started to pray . . . and other changes followed. I heard the story a long while after it happened, but I didn't want ha-Shem to need to send anything like that to me. Hearing the story was enough to make me want

*to change, to turn my heart around and make me desire a re-
lationship with God.*

*Nobody likes restrictions, and perhaps that's why we re-
sist growing. We don't like anyone telling us what we can and
can't do. We like to do what we feel makes sense. Maybe it's
not my place to tell all of you this. I "woke up" less than a year
ago. I started learning only ten months ago. I'm not even an in-
fant. But it is [my place]. Someone in my place is the only one
[who] really can [tell you]. Why? Because I've been there and
I've been here. I know what it's like to not know better. One year
ago, I didn't know better. I know what it's like in both places; I
know what it's like to not want to be burdened with obligations. I know what it's like to want to feel free and not be riddled with guilt. I started off in one place and I'm growing
toward another. I'm looking ahead. This direction is better. Doing more of what ha-Shem wants feels much much better.*

—Victoria, twenty-four, New York

Still, faith in God is not a requirement for accepting Judaism
into our lives. If we study the teachings from a secular point of
view, we may see the system of values and ethics that emerges
and begin to appreciate the community we once rejected or took
for granted. "Working in the Jewish community," Marlene says,
"I have become more aware of issues that affect us, politically,
socially, economically—and I care more deeply about them."

We may even decide that we want to share our lives with
someone who sees the wisdom of Jewish ways and shares our
fondness for Judaism's culture and tradition. Jeff, a thirty-four-
year-old Jewish psychologist from Philadelphia, explains: "Pre-
viously, numerous girlfriends were all non-Jewish. I decided I'd
like to marry a Jew, so now I date only Jewish women. Not
because of religion so much as culture. I sum it up as 'you don't
have to explain what gefilte fish is!'"

## WE REAFFIRM OUR PRE-EXISTING BELIEFS

Some SJFs never develop any feelings for Judaism. At sixty, Diana has been through more than enough of life's stages to know that she is indeed a devout atheist. "I never had any desire to get in touch with my Jewish identity," Diana told me. "I feel more American than Jewish. Really, I feel I am a New York Jew like both my parents were. Growing up, I went to two Reform Sunday schools, which taught me nothing. Even before I met my husband, who is Modern Orthodox, religion did not interest me. Boring and irrelevant and really a man-made institution. Before I first married twenty years ago, I felt quite alone as a hybrid, sort of between the religious and the non, neither of whom fully understood me."

Conversely, SJFs who grew up with a strong sense of Jewish identity but casually dated non-Jews often stop pursuing these relationships around the time we start thinking seriously about the next step—marriage and children. Many become even more involved in their respective Jewish communities and restrict their dating accordingly. "I am ready to settle down," says Jenny, a thirty-year-old marketing executive from Los Angeles. "But I've found that my non-Jewish boyfriends could never share my love for Jewish tradition. So now I date only other Jews."

## WE VACILLATE BACK AND FORTH

Since morphing into our adult selves can take years, many of us find that our beliefs fluctuate over the course of the transition. One year, we're committed to perpetuating the Jewish people by dating only among the Chosen, the next, we're feeling the spirit of universalism and embracing multiculturalism and all its implications. Take SJF Sharone, for example:

*I have dated plenty of non-Jewish men. Over the past couple of years I have decided that I wanted to date only Jewish men because I am more serious regarding dating and relationships. Meaning that if it should turn into something serious it would be with somebody Jewish. My parents have always asked me to date Jewish men and a large part of me does it just for them.*

*However, I have just recently met somebody that I really like, which so rarely happens. But he is not Jewish. I am tired of limiting myself and I am an adult now. I do not think my religion plays a strong enough role in my life to limit myself to a large part of the male population. I am currently twenty-six years old, what if I end up spending my life alone simply because I have not met a Jewish man who suits my needs. And for what, for my parents? What about my life? I have to live it. My attitude has changed. My connection to the religion lessens with time. I don't so much agree with religion. Any religion. It is cultish. However, I do appreciate tradition and I think that is helpful for a familial structure.*

—Sharone, twenty-six, New York

Such changes are completely natural. The key is to accept these inconsistencies as an organic part of the growth process. We all contend with the same confusion, entertain the same doubts, and fight the same fears. In the end, the best any one of us can do is what feels right.

## WE TURN AWAY FROM ALL RELIGION
## IN FAVOR OF PERSONAL SPIRITUALITY

Maturing into adults and shedding the last remnants of childhood is hard enough all on its own. In the wake of the World Trade Center tragedy, however, many of us have had to take a giant leap to the next level . . . coming face to face with death and our own mortality. Simultaneously, we've also seen the destruction that any religion can wreak when taken to a militant extreme. Is there any wonder that so many of us have decided to embrace the universalist and humanist ethic?

*After September 11th, I began to feel that group identity, as a Jew, as a Muslim, as an American, even as a woman, as any "category" one puts oneself in, is dividing us, repressing our inner selves, destroying our world, and keeping us from expressing the identities that really matter: our own wholly individual identity, and the identity we share with everyone in the world—our identity as human beings. Considering one's shared identity with others as human beings is a greater moral safeguard than all the thousands of rules of a thousand religions have ever been.*

—Marcy, twenty-six, Los Angeles

*As I get older, I've become less concerned about dating Jews. I'm more selective on my girlfriends' values and motivations in life, less selective on their political, religious views. To be honest, with the way things are in the world these days, if I find someone with similar ethics and morals and there is love in the house, but they're not Jewish, I'm still gonna date them.*

—Michael, thirty, Cleveland, Ohio

When all is said and done, we come back to the original point: There is no right or wrong way to be Jewish. If we enter marriage with our eyes open, the views we take on around this time of personal transformation will be with us for many years to come. Our values and morals will lend structure to our lives and give us the strength to raise our children. These are years of great self-exploration: We must make the most of them, no matter where they may lead us.

## THE LAST WORD

Few of us are so hardheaded as to insist that being Jewish has absolutely no effect on our perspective. In some way, shape, or form, our identity as Jews informs much of our lives. From birth to marriage to death, we find that our relationship to Judaism evolves in fascinating and often surprising ways. As we exit childhood and embark on the adulthood that is so often associated with marriage and parenthood, we start looking for truth, meaning, and a new way to lead our lives.

Some of us will find what we are looking for early on, either through Jewish religion, culture, or community. Others may return later in life. And still others may never know what it is to participate in Jewish life as adults. While we're dating and trying to decide on the role Judaism will play in our future, we may want to take the time to learn as much as possible about the Jewish people and way of life. Toward that end, you may want to check out Additional Resources (on page 179).

# chapter two

## Where the Jewish Boys Are

*I date only Jews. I won't even agree to a date with someone who isn't Jewish. It's not that I have anything against non-Jews, but my parents are Holocaust survivors. It's different when you know that someone actually tried to kill you just because you are Jewish. I feel a tremendous sense of responsibility that goes beyond reason. If I'm going to get married, my husband will have to be Jewish.*

*—Rachel, thirty-six, Brooklyn*

For some Jewish women, the question is not should I date a Jewish man, but where and how can I meet one? Some of us have developed a strong personal relationship with Judaism, having rediscovered the beauty and spirit of the tradition on our own. In the process, we gained a sense of peace and connectedness to our people, our past, and our future. We've become well versed in the teachings of our faith, and now that we are of age, we can think of no greater gift to pass on to our children.

A connection to Jewish tradition, however, is not the sole reason some SJFs choose to stick with the J-crew. Many of us grew up surrounded by non-Jews. Our sense of Jewish identity was foisted on us by our minority status. As many Jews will attest, you never feel quite as Jewish in New York as you do in Des Moines. For those of us who grew up feeling like so many ugly ducklings because of our religion, finding a community of Jewish swans awaiting us with open wings can come as a tremendous relief.

Then there are women like Rachel. SJFs with family who nearly perished in the Holocaust. SJFs who face the pain of past persecution every time they look in the eyes of their parents or grandparents. These women are not so far removed from history that they can treat their Jewishness as a nonissue. For them, dating a gentile isn't even an option. It's not personal, it's not rational, it's not even a matter of choice.

Whatever our reasons, we're no longer looking at dating as a way to pass the time, but as a means to an end—that end being a Jewish wedding ( *Jewish* being the operative word). To hear many SJFs tell it, meeting Jewish guys was easy during our younger years. We danced our first "Havah Nagilah" with them at Bar and Bat Mitzvahs, we shared our first kisses with them during summers at Camp Chippewa, and we recognized them from a mile away by the Jewish fraternity letters emblazoned on their sweatshirts in college.

*The closest I ever came to dating a Jewish boy was in eighth grade. But how well does one date when they are thirteen years old? Not very well, since I broke up with him after having to kiss him for the first time because it scared me.*

*—Randi, twenty-six, Chicago*

*My parents sent me to an all-Jewish sleep-away camp when I was eleven, twelve, and thirteen years old. The first boy I ever kissed was Jewish! I dated Jewish boys at camp, but again, I was just a kid. I have not dated any Jewish boys since.*

*—Lena, twenty-three, Paramus, New Jersey*

*I do not attend synagogue. But one of my first boyfriends at age sixteen, I met at synagogue. But that was the only time I met a guy at synagogue.*

*—Valerie, twenty-seven, Santa Monica, California*

*My very first Jewish boyfriend was at age sixteen, we were working together on a summer trip to Nevada. That was pretty easy because it was a Jewish organized trip.*

*—Sandy, twenty-four, Boston*

*I dated three Jewish guys just in my first semester at Kansas University. We had so many to choose from, I couldn't make up my mind. Every bar I went to was packed with Jewish guys. I think I took it for granted that there would always be plenty to go around.*

*—Heather, thirty-three, St. Louis*

Yes, those were the days. But now that all the organized Jewish activity is over and the pickings are slim, we may be kicking ourselves in the heinie for missing out on all the hot J-boy action. Why, oh why, weren't we ready to commit back then? When dating Jewish guys was about as challenging as finding a synagogue in Manhattan? Oh, to be twelve again!

Okay, so maybe we're not as broken up about it as all that, but many of us are confused. Where are all the single Jewish boys hiding? Are there any good ones left? And if there are, why aren't we meeting the little buggers? What's a well-meaning Jewish girl to do? The answers are all in this chapter. Some of the topics covered in the following pages are

- Ways to increase your chances of meeting an SJM.

- The role of friends and family in helping you meet the Jewish man of your dreams.

- The best match-making and dating services to expand your options.

- How you can meet Jewish men without going out of your way.

- Cities with the largest Jewish populations.

**GOOD J-DAR: YOU EITHER HAVE IT OR YOU DON'T**

*How do I manage to restrict my dating to Jewish men? Simple: attraction. I'm not usually attracted to non-Jews. It must have something to do with my fetish for nerdy Jewish guys with curly hair, glasses, cuteness, huggability, constant jokes, and a huge brain. Jewish men can talk about feelings, be intimate—they seem more like "normal people" from a girl's perspective than some perfectly sculpted jock with a macho stick up his ass. However, they can also be big whiny babies who require a lot of work from hardheaded Jewish women for emotional upkeep. But for me, the rewards outweigh the drawbacks.*

—Lisa, twenty-seven, San Diego

For Lisa, dating Jewish guys is only natural. She is drawn to everything about them. Furthermore, she's gone so far as to associate non-Jewish guys with predominantly negative character traits. Although she's explained that she does appreciate her friendships with non-Jews, saying that "it's fun to explore our different cultures," her state of mind is such that she will no doubt enjoy a bright, menorah-candle-lighting future for many years to come.

Good J-dar is the reason women like Lisa are never at a loss for available Jewish men while other SJFs can't seem to catch a break. Whether at a party, at the office, or on the beach, the J-dar-packing SJF can home in on the only Jewish guy within a five-mile radius and strike up a meaningful conversation within minutes. If you're reading this chapter, looking for bigger and better ways to meet your Kosher-keeping honey, chances are your J-dar is not all that it can be.

> I have not met any attractive Jewish guys since high school. I have friends with cute Jewish boyfriends, but the only ones I seem to meet are not my type. Sometimes I think all the good Jews are taken. A few months ago, I finally met a guy I thought was both attractive and Jewish. I was so sure he was Jewish, I even asked him about his Bar Mitzvah. I was really embarrassed when he didn't know what I was talking about.
>
> —Brie, twenty-eight, Los Angeles

Without good J-dar, you're stuck having to figure out the details for yourself. Here are some questions to help you find out if the guy you've set your sights on meets the rabbinical requirements:

- *What's your name?* It's safe to say that 99 percent of all Aris and Elis are Jewish. The same goes for common Israeli names like Ronen and Yaron. David is also popular among our people. If you meet a Colin or a Chris, the chance of Hebrew ancestry is slim. Brians, Jasons, Gregs, and most other first names can go either way.

• *What's your last name?* This is almost as effective as asking, "When is your birthday?" if you want to find out someone's astrological sign. Cohens, Shapiros, Siegels and anything with a "man," "stein," "feld," or "berg" as a suffix spell J-E-W. Millers and Greens are tricky, so prepare to do more digging. Anything featuring two capital letters and begins with a Mac or Van is out of bounds (but don't despair . . . follow-up questions may reveal that their mothers are Jewish). Guys who look Jewish, but whose last names end with a vowel are probably just Italian. Close, but definitely no cigar.

• *What's your ethnic background?* Most Jewish guys won't beat around the burning bush. They'll tell you straight out . . . I'm a German/Russian/Polish Jew. Or they'll say they're Israeli and put all doubt to rest. If they don't identify themselves as Jewish, all is not lost. Follow-up questions like "Why did your ancestors emigrate from the old country?" may yield more concrete results.

• *Are you/your parents Catholic?* Take this roundabout approach when you don't want to seem obvious. If a guy tells you he's French or Spanish, follow up with the Catholic question. Dutchmen and Germans get the Lutheran query. Explain that you're only asking because you're interested in national religions. This rationale should allay any worries they may have about you sizing them up for a groom's tux.

• *So, are you Jewish or what?* If your subject has expertly evaded all of your questions and you have nothing against the direct approach, now would be the time to employ it . . . at your own risk, of course. Then again, any SJM who has a problem with an SJF who knows what she wants is probably not your Jewish American Prince Charming anyway.

*Sometimes, I'll be at a bar with my friends and I'll meet a guy. We'll be talking and the more attracted I become, the more I'll start wondering whether he's Jewish. It makes it really hard to focus on the conversation, because the whole time, I'm thinking, "I hope he's Jewish. How do I find out?"*

—Stacey, twenty-five, Farmington Hills

## KEEPING THE FAITH: DISCRIMINATING DATERS

*My cousin and one of my best friends were both in serious relationships with non-Jews (my cousin was engaged to a Catholic Cuban girl, my best friend dated a Catholic guy for three years) and both ended badly because of differences stemming from each one's desire to keep hold of their religion. That put me off interfaith dating even more. I never even considered the possibility of dating someone outside the Jewish faith. I never accepted a date with a non-Jew, never let anyone fix me up with one, and never even gave my number out. I didn't want to put myself in a position of having to choose.*

—Jamie, twenty-seven, Miami

Being a discriminating dater is never simple. Not for us the easy lure of someone who is ready, willing, and able. We want more. We need sparks. We look for chemistry. We yearn for that special feeling. Otherwise, the jig is up. Yes, it's not easy being picky. But being a Jewish discriminating dater is ever tougher. If finding chemistry and attraction weren't hard enough, they must now come with a *mohel*-circumcized package. How does anyone manage? Here are a few tips gleaned from Jewish gals just like you:

- *Just say no:* If you've come to a point in your life at which you know that you simply cannot get serious about anyone

## JEWISH ENOUGH?

You say you're serious about marrying a Jew, but what does that mean, exactly? Did you know that according to Orthodox Jewish law, half-Jewish is the same as half-pregnant—an impossibility. You're either in or you're out. While we may all have our personal definitions of Jews and gentiles, there is no gray area in the eyes of Orthodox Jewish law, which defines a Jew as anyone:

- Who was born to a Jewish mother.

- Whose mother underwent an Orthodox Jewish conversion before their birth.

- Who has undergone an Orthodox Jewish conversion (As of this writing, those who convert under the auspices of a Reform or Conservative rabbi are not considered Jewish by the Orthodox).

So, how Jewish is Jewish enough for you? While the less stringent movements recognize Jews with Jewish fathers and gentile mothers, the Orthodox streams are sticklers for the rules. So, someone who is one-sixteenth Jewish can be considered a full-blooded Jew whereas someone who is three-quarters Jewish can be considered a gentile. How can this be possible? Here's how it works:

A Jewish woman marries a gentile. They have a daughter. By Orthodox Jewish law, she is considered Jewish. By any other standard, half-Jewish. If she marries a gentile and has a daughter of her own, the rest of the world would see said daughter as only a quarter Jewish, but she would be a full Jew according to Jewish law. She, in turn, marries a gentile and gives birth to a daughter as well. While this child is only one-eighth Jewish by most yardsticks, she is a full Jew according to Jewish tradition. Naturally, if she too marries a gentile, her children will all be considered Jewish by the Orthodox school, while most people would say the kids are one-sixteenth Jewish.

Meanwhile, anyone whose mother isn't Jewish is a non-Jew. So even if three out of your four grandparents are Jewish with the exception of your maternal grandmother, you are not officially a Jew, while someone who technically has only one Jewish great-great-grandmother can qualify as a full Jew. The law creates many strange situations. For instance, lifelong Jews who go to temple and keep all the traditions may not be "really" Jewish, while those who take weekly communion, give up red meat for Lent and have a Jewish ancestor they've only heard stories about can be considered full-fledged Jews.

who is not of the Jewish persuasion, then you need to get comfortable doling out rejection. Remember, every time you go on a date or start a relationship with a non-Jew, you shut out opportunities to meet a perfectly suitable Jewish guy.

*A few months ago, I realized that I may be dating non-Jewish women because I'm not ready for a serious commitment. This was fine when I was twenty-five, but now that I'm thirty-one, I am beginning to reevaluate. When I think about possibly getting married and building a future with someone, I think of doing that with someone Jewish. It's odd that I started thinking about that only now.*

*—Drew, thirty-one, New York*

• *Be your own boss:* If you've made a rule for yourself, hold yourself accountable. The decision to stay in the fold is never easy. For many of us, the choice may even involve ending previous relationships and reevaluating our purpose in life. But the second we think that the hard part is behind us, we run the risk of being taken unawares by a new and improved temptation designed to steer us off our chosen course. Remember, restricting yourself to Jews gets easier only after you're married to one. Until such time, vigilance is key. To hold fast to your goals, you'll need to keep them at the forefront of your mind. Follow the tips in this chapter to stay focused.

• *Keep faith alive:* If you are single and looking, there are only two things that will help you say no to an attractive non-Jew in need of your phone number. These are the determination to wind up with a Jew and the faith that it can happen to you. Believe it or not, there are plenty of Jewish guys to go around. No matter what city you call home. After meeting one too many disappointing Jewish prospects, many of us get dejected. We may even give up hope of ever finding the right Jewish guy. But while the fact that in life there are no guarantees may stop some people from holding fast to their beliefs, we Jews have had thousands of years to practice keeping faith alive. Centuries upon centuries of religious persecution have created a group of people bred to hold fast to their ideals or die trying. So just because you haven't met the Jewish man of your dreams just yet, don't give up. It takes only one day, one Jew, one introduction to change everything.

## OUT AND ABOUT:
## THE KOSHER MEAT MARTS

*I think the best place to meet fellow Jews has to be through friends. I have met all of my boyfriends that way—never on an actual fix-up, just by being out at a party, bar, or restaurant with people who knew people who knew other people, etc. . . . My last Jewish boyfriend, I met at a party on a rooftop in Manhattan. It was my good friend's birthday party and almost everyone there had gone to college together except me. I hadn't met a lot of the guys who showed up and one caught my attention. I asked my friend to introduce me when he came by. She did, and we dated for six months.*

*The one before that was pretty similar. He was the roommate of a guy that I knew and we would run into each other a lot at dinners, parties, going out. After a few run-ins we both mentioned to mutual friends that we were interested and ended up dating for a year and a half.*

*—Andi, twenty-six, New York*

Faith and determination are important, but as Andi's example shows, SJFs who involve themselves in social situations with SJMs need not rely exclusively on optimism to see them through. With the right attitude and good connections, you'll soon have nice Jewish boys coming out of your ears.

As you probably already know, meeting new people requires a certain kind of energy. Being out and about is not enough . . . the right frame of mind is everything. No matter who you encounter, a good mood, a positive outlook, and an open disposition can go a long way. The following are great places to meet fellow Jews when you're going out and outgoing:

- *Parties:* What better place to meet someone than at a friend's party? You can set your sites on a new guy, orchestrate an introduction, engage in a heart-to-heart, and even hear about his relationship history from his friends and exes—all in the span of one night.

- *Bars:* Many women will insist that a bar is the last place on earth to meet anyone serious. Don't you believe them.

Just talk to any straight, single Jewish guy and he'll tell you flat out: "I met my last two girlfriends at a bar," says Scott, a twenty-nine-year-old SJM from Minneapolis. "It's much easier to get to know people after they've had a drink and their inhibitions are down. I've found that women are more relaxed at bars. And that makes me more relaxed. That and the drinks."

• *Weddings:* The benefits are the same as the kind you'll find at a regular party, except a wedding comes with one major bonus—the atmosphere is designed expressly to idealize and romanticize relationships. To make the situation even more auspicious, weddings remind guys that pretty soon, they'll be the only single swinging from the vine and that maybe it's time to think ahead. If that's your intention as well, prepare for a meeting of the minds.

• *Synagogue:* This is in no way intended to suggest that you go out and join a temple just to meet a Jewish guy. Bad idea. However, if you already belong to a synagogue or want to join up for your own spiritual and religious reasons, do not discount the romantic potential. Saturday morning luncheons offer plenty of socializing opportunity to go along with those free mini-bagels and kosher brownies. If you spot a cute guy sitting two rows ahead of you, approach him after services when the air is ripe with possibility and people are feeling friendly. Ask him if he's new, ask him if he likes the rabbi, ask him his name. It doesn't matter what you ask, as long as you get the conversation under way.

• *The JCC:* If you live close to a Jewish Community Center, you're in luck. JCCs offer a wealth of activities. You can meet Jews in photography class or while doing the Downward Dog in the yoga studio. Of course, if you'd rather meet

Jewish men the old-fashioned way, JCCs also stage many events for singles.

• *Bar and Bat Mitzvahs:* Can you say wall-to-wall Jews? Although most of these people will be kids and parents, the imbalance can work in your favor when Aunt Claire introduces you to one of the only young, single guys in the room. If he turns out to be a shmuck, don't kvetch. Keep shmoozing and you'll go home with a wallet full of business cards from people just dying to set up a nice meydl like yourself.

• *Fix-ups:* Not to belabor the point, but as I already mentioned, when it comes to match making, Jews are completely out of control. Everyone from your mother to your friends to your real estate agent can and will try to pair you off. Embrace these opportunities no matter how picky you think you are. If you think of fix-ups as the dreaded "f-word" and can't seem to reconcile yourself to the concept, check out the tips in the "Just Looking: Your Guide to Blind Dating" on page 37.

## MORE, MORE, MORE: EXPANDING YOUR OPTIONS

*I first signed up with JDate after breaking up with my non-Jewish boyfriend. I had decided that I could not marry a non-Jew. I need to be with someone who will take an equal role in developing my children's Jewish identity. That's why JDate. I have a lot of Jewish friends, but getting back into the dating scene wasn't easy and JDate gave me a great jump-start. Looking at all the letters that poured into my in-box was a tremendous ego boost. I was dating all the time.*

*Last year, after going out with what felt like a million guys,*

## JUST LOOKING:
## YOUR GUIDE TO BLIND DATING

Many SJFs in search of their male counterparts do themselves a grave disservice by consistently rejecting their friends' and relatives' attempts at match making. For many, going on a blind date is tantamount to admitting that they can't get action on their own. Others simply think of the process as a long and painful death. If you fall into either of these categories or have come up with yet another reason to just say no, the following tips may help you get over your issues and get in the swing of blind dating:

• *Just drinks:* Dinner, movies, and bowling are inappropriate for a blind date. You've never met this person before, so keep the initial meeting casual. Think short and noncommittal. Drinks at a local watering hole or a cup of coffee at the corner Starbucks should provide you with all the time you need to figure out if you're interested. And don't feel guilty about cutting the date short, either. What nicer, more tactful way to let him know he shouldn't bother with any follow-up calls?

• *Just conversation:* Going into a fix-up with great expectations is the surest way to end up disappointed. Chances of your date being "the one" are slim to none, so don't stress out too much over your hair, your clothes, your make-up, your mani-pedi, or any other aspect of predate preparation. The most you can expect is a chance to talk to a new person, express your views, and hear what they have to say for themselves.

• *Just friends:* Many people think that blind dates are awkward because they're expected to be attracted to one another. Cross that theory off your list right now. Instead of sitting across the table, thinking

"I can't believe they thought I'd be perfect for this guy! I hope he doesn't think I'm interested in him," look at it as a chance to meet a person you wouldn't get to know under ordinary circumstances. Pick his brain, find out what makes him tick, and walk away with a new friend—or at the very least, a positive experience.

*I finally met someone special. We've been together ever since and are engaged to be married next spring.*

—*Lilah, twenty-eight, Chicago*

In the age of technology, we now have dating down to a science. Just because no one strikes your fancy at the local shul and you can't seem to meet a Jew to save your life doesn't mean that you're on a one-way track to interfaith romance. The power to date Jewish is completely in your hands. You need only learn how to use it.

If you are truly serious about dating Jews, your first step should be to put down this book, get off your couch, and walk over to your computer. If you don't have one at home, use the one at the office (provided of course, your cyber-activity is not closely monitored by the brass). Open your web browser and type in JDate.com, match.com, personals.nerve.com, SpeedDating.com, or HurryDate.com, and behold as an entire world of romantic opportunity unfolds before your very eyes.

*I've never tried JDate, SpeedDating, or any service. I hate these things. They turn love into a job interview. Can you imagine telling your children the story of how you met—how romantic, we found out over the computer that we had similar goals. Blech. Life is life, not business.*

—*Jodi, twenty-six, Boca Raton*

If you're thinking, "You tell her, Jodi! Me? Internet date? Never!" may I suggest an attitude adjustment? Three reasons: First, don't knock it till you've tried it. Many women have had great dating experiences on the 'Net. And no, they're not unattractive, friendless, or otherwise impaired! (I know what you're thinking!) Some, like Lilah whose story began this section, have even fallen in love and gotten engaged.

Second, get with the times. Gone are the days when Internet dating was the sole province of the socially awkward and people had to conceal their JDate membership like a zit on a first date. Today, JDate alone boasts millions of quality, Jewish singles looking to connect with someone compatible. Nothing wrong with those odds.

Finally, remember, if God had meant for us to meet on the subway, He wouldn't have created computers. In the quest to meet new people and make productive use of our time, we'd be foolish not to employ all the resources at our disposal. Here is a partial list and a description of the types of services available:

- *JDate:* This is the granddaddy of all Jewish-dating Web sites. JDate enables users to search the globe for single Jews. If you haven't already joined or at least heard of JDate, you're in for quite a shock. American Jews, Israeli Jews, South American Jews, take your pick, they're all on www.JDate.com. Orthodox, Conservative, Reform, secular . . . here they are, in all their Jewish glory. You can look at their pictures, read their carefully crafted profiles, and even chat via instant messaging functions. Soon enough, you'll figure out why there seem to be less and less Jewish guys to go around: Apparently, they're all at home, glued to their computers. For tips on how to make the most out of JDate and similar sites, check out "Cyber Loving" on page 41. Other Jewish dating sites of interest: Jmatch.com, JewishCafe.com

• *Other Dating Sites:* While there is a preponderance of Web sites geared toward helping the lovelorn, three of the most popular that also allow you to check for religious background are match.com, personals.nerve.com, and GreatBoyfriends.com. As the site that boasts the most members, match.com is the hands-down winner in the popularity contest. A few minutes there, and you'll be tapping your foot to the beat of "so many men, so little time." However, nerve.com distinguishes itself on the basis of quality rather than quantity. Suffice to say that it's the dating site for people who wouldn't be caught dead on a dating site. Now then, if you're looking for a guy who comes with references, GreatBoyfriends.com is for you. Here, women post pictures of their ex-boyfriends (or in some cases, their brothers, friends, sons, and co-workers) and tell you why the guy is such a great catch. Best of all, you can e-mail the women directly and ask them anything you'd like to know about the man who caught your eye.

*I think JDate and all Internet dating sites need to come with a warning. As in, "Warning: Your dates can and will use this site against you." I met this guy through JDate last year. We were dating for a couple of months, but not exclusively. I didn't tell him that I was seeing other people, and he never asked. Instead, he created all these aliases and started e-mailing me to see if I would respond. I got stood up on three dates before I put two and two together, when he let slip that he knew I had plans before I'd even said anything. I was really mad. Ever since then, I won't make a date with a guy without talking on the phone first. Even then, I'm still paranoid it's some guy I dated disguising his voice.*

*—Jennifer, twenty-five, Baltimore*

# CYBER LOVING

Online dating seems easy enough. Ostensibly, all that is required is that you create a profile by answering a few straightforward questions and uploading your photo. Then, kick back, relax, and wait for them to come to you. Of course, few things are as simple as they sound . . . and online dating is no exception. Whether you are new to the Internet dating game or just need to brush up on your skills, the following tips and anecdotes should prove to be of assistance.

## WHO AM I?

Sample profile:

"I'm down-to-earth, adventurous, outgoing, intelligent, spontaneous, energetic, spiritual, caring, and fun-loving."

**Q: Why does the above description fall short of the mark?**

**A:** When you are writing your profile, steer clear of long-winded sentences that pile one adjective upon the next. Why? Here's one adjective for you: Boring. Instead, get personal. Give concrete examples from your life, something they can sink their teeth into. When it comes to profiles, specifics rule. What else is going to make your profile stand out from the next? Obviously, crafting a one-of-a-kind profile will take some effort on your part. You'll need to think about what makes you unique. One quick way to come up with a bunch of great ideas is to take a moment to look at yourself through the eyes of your friends and smitten ex-boyfriends. What do all these people love about you? Figure it out, then write it down.

Better profile:

"The first thing you'll notice about me is my energy. I have a lot to go around, so chances are you'll never be bored with me. I know how to have a good time, but I also have a serious side. As my friends and family know, relationships are very important to me and I don't treat them lightly. People often ask why I'm single. The truth is, I have more fun being by myself than with the wrong person . . . yes, I just haven't met the right guy yet."

## GETTING TO KNOW YOU

"I've been e-mailing this guy from match.com for two weeks. He's very cool. His e-mails are so funny. Yesterday, we spoke on the phone for the first time. I hope he calls again.

—Leah, thirty-two, New York

### Q: What is Leah doing wrong?

**A:** Truth be told, the above Leah is none other than yours truly. Sadly, dating experts are not born but made through one learning experience after another. So when I first got up the nerve to check out the on-line dating scene, I regularly engaged in these relatively long-term e-mail and phone relationships. I'd feel all the anxiety that usually accompanies a burgeoning romance. Then I'd finally meet the guy and watch as my heart dropped like the New Year's ball in Time Square. Moral of the story: Keep the predate warmup as short as possible. No use in getting your hopes up over what could very well be nothing.

## GREAT EXPECTATIONS

I'm going on my first JDate. I am so excited. He's so cute in his picture. Plus, he told me that he lives on the Gold Coast. He's got a duplex in a brownstone just off Lake Shore Drive. He's a doctor. I can't wait to meet him."
—Janice, thirty-three, Chicago

**Q:** What's wrong with Janice's note?

**A:** Janice is too excited. She is likely to be disappointed. Never, ever get this giddy about anyone whom you have yet to meet. I know, it can be tempting. You look at his picture and his green eyes beckon to you. You feel the rush of hormones and start feeling just like a schoolgirl. "Will he call? When? Please, God let it be soon." When these feelings start to creep up, as they invariably will in your first flush of online romance, keep the following in mind: (1) the most popular gripe about the Internet is "the pictures are not representative" and (2) you'll often have more chemistry with the photos and profiles on the sites than with the people these photos and profiles represent.

• *SpeedDating:* Believe it or not, the SpeedDating phenomenon sweeping the globe was actually started by Jews. Concerned by the high intermarriage statistics among U.S. Jews, a Jewish educational group came up with this groundbreaking idea and called it "SpeedDating." Here's how it works: Seven tables are set up. One woman and one man are assigned to each table. The event organizer rings a bell and the chitchat begins. After seven minutes of conversation, the bell rings again. Besides serving as a signal for the men to move on, the bell also signifies the moment of truth. Now that you've had seven minutes to get to know each other, what do you think? A scorecard allows participants to discretely mark "yes" or "no." When both people mark "yes," that's a match. Everyone makes his or her choice, then each SJM stands and moves on to the next SJF. At the end of the night, people turn in their scorecards. Within two days, participants receive e-mail notification of their matches along with said matches' contact information.

*I went to HurryDate with my best friend. Talk about a "Speed-Dating don't." I know it may seem scary to go alone, but take my word, it's worse when you take a close friend of the same sex. After we got the results back, I was so mad. Not only did she have more matches than me but she had them with some of the guys that I liked . . . guys who didn't pick me! I know it's immature, but I wouldn't talk to her for a week after. I just couldn't get over it. I joke about it, but my ego still hasn't recovered.*

—Lisa, twenty-nine, New York

• *HurryDate and 8minuteDating:* While SpeedDating is exclusively and rigorously Jewish, requiring participants to either have been born Jewish (that is, to a Jewish mother) or to have undergone an Orthodox conversion, HurryDate and 8minuteDating are the equal-opportunity date parties that let you choose whether you want to mingle with the general population and ferret out the Jews for yourself or attend one of their strictly Jewish events. The 8minuteDating service is nearly an exact replica of SpeedDating. The only difference is that there are eight couples instead of seven, and people spend eight minutes speaking before making their final decision. HurryDate, on the other hand, takes the SpeedDating idea to the extreme. When they say, "Dating should be fun and in mass quantities," they're not joking. A grand total of twenty-five introductions are made in the course of every evening.

How do they do it? Simple. You have only three minutes to get to know each person. Talk about a mind scramble.

---

## THE NEED FOR SPEED

If you want to win hearts on your SpeedDating expedition, you'll need to come prepared. As always, the right attitude is everything. The following pointers will ensure that you're feeling your best—no matter how high pressure the situation:

• *Rest up:* Try to spend your day without exerting too much energy. This goes double if you're headed for a HurryDate. Twenty-five conversations within the span of ninety minutes will tax even the most outgoing of you. So, if you can, prepare by keeping a vow of silence all day. On second thought, consider zipping it for an entire week.

• *Feel your best:* Wear your favorite outfit. Get your hair done. Sing yourself a love song before you leave the house. Remember, love yourself and the men will follow.

• *Relax:* This is not a test. Repeat, this is not a test. No need to stress out or worry too much about the impression you're making. Focus on getting to know the person seated directly across from you.

• *Flirt:* There's nothing more attractive than a flirty woman. So turn on the charm and use the feminine wiles *ha-Shem* gave you. Smile, hold his gaze, touch his hand and, by all means, be yourself. They'll eat it up.

• *Inquire:* Never mind what these guys do for a living, find out what's going on in their lives, why they decided to go SpeedDating and what gives their life meaning. It's a tall order for three to eight minutes, but if you can get into their heads, you'll make wiser decisions.

---

## *TIKUN OLAM:* GIVE AND YOU SHALL RECEIVE

*Last spring, I went to a pro-Israel rally in Washington, D.C. It was my first time taking part in a demonstration. When I got to the synagogue where we were all supposed to meet and get on the bus, I immediately noticed a cute guy. Right there, I decided I would sit next to him. We talked all the way through the four-hour bus ride. I loved that he had such a strong social conscience and felt so strongly about Israel.*

*By the time we got to D.C., we'd already exchanged phone numbers and felt like old friends. We had our first date within two days of the rally. Now we're living together.*

—Jennifer, twenty-five, Philadelphia

Going out with the intention of meeting new people is all well and good, but you can spend only so much time on the pursuit of a Jewish guy without starting to feel like, well, like you've got nothing better to do with your life. *Tikun olam,* which means "healing the world" in Hebrew, is one of the central tenets of Judaism. Volunteering your time and energy to worthwhile Jewish causes is the single best way to meet Jewish men while contributing to society.

The benefits of volunteer work go way beyond filling up your Palm Pilot with the names of new friends and potential boyfriends. No matter what kind of project you choose to take on, you'll know that you're helping out and making a difference. The rewards of doing *tzedakah* (that's "good deeds" for those of you who zoned out in Hebrew school) will come in the form of increased self-esteem as well as newfound passions and interests (not just in the romantic sense).

Before you start looking into the many available volunteer

opportunities, take some time to think about what kind of work would be the most enriching to you. Volunteer initiatives fall into the following two categories:

• *Political activism:* Nothing beats political activism when you want to effect change on a grand scale. Whether your interest is in American–Israeli relations, Jews of the Diaspora, or the state of Jews right here in the United States, you can be sure that there is a campaign to promote your interests. Going on rallies will enable you to bond over a common cause with hundreds of Jews, while helping organize events and working the phones during telethons will ensure that you work closely with like-minded people and possibly meet someone you like in the process.

• *Humanitarian efforts:* Jewish organizations like the United Jewish Federation always need volunteers to act locally. The federation, for instance, offers many different types of volunteer opportunities. You can choose them based on your area of interest, the time commitment required, and the location of the job. Onetime events, such as coat drives, holiday gift wrapping, and seders often mean that you'll be working with many SJMs from your area.

## BACK TO SCHOOL: THE LEARNING CONNECTION

*When I was younger, I wasn't the least bit interested in Judaism or going to temple. I was sure that bars and parties were the best places to meet guys. Now, I see it completely differently. Over the years, I've become a lot more Jewish. I still won't keep kosher, but I do go to temple, and I've been taking classes to learn more about the religion and tradition. Even*

## VOLUNTEER ORGANIZATIONS

If you'd like to volunteer but don't know where to begin, check out the following Web sites and organizations:

• There is a Jewish Federation in every major U.S. city. To find the one in your area, just go to your favorite search engine and type in the name of your hometown followed by the words "Jewish Federation." Then go to the site and click on the link for volunteering or getting involved. These sites offer many opportunities for local volunteer work.

• United Jewish Communities is the umbrella organization that supports the Jewish Federations of North America. Go to www.ujc.com and click on SOCIAL ACTION/HELP OTHERS and you'll find out how to get involved in working for Jews on a national level.

• American Jewish World Service is a site for American Jews who want to do some good in other parts of the world (www.ajws.org). Global action involves doing volunteer work in countries like South America, Russia, Ukraine, Africa, and Asia. Assignments last anywhere from one month to one year. If you've ever considered breaking out of your routine and opening yourself up to completely new experiences, this organization may be exactly what you need.

• **The Jewish SuperSite:** If you'd like to see what other options are available to you, go to www.zipple.com and click on NOT-FOR-PROFIT. The site will provide you with many links to volunteer organizations all over the United States and abroad.

*though there are more women than men in these classes, I've had a lot in common with many of the men I met.*

*—Abby, thirty-four, Dallas*

In the name of meeting men while pursuing other interests and not at their expense, some SJFs choose to combine their love of learning with their love of SJMs by taking Jewish-oriented courses. If you're curious about any aspect of Judaism, you can attend a class or a lecture. In so doing, you'll broaden your understanding and meet Jewish men with whom you're guaranteed to have at least one interest in common.

When it comes to delving deeper into Judaism, there is no shortage of avenues to explore. Here are just a couple of subjects you may want to study:

- *Hebrew:* If you're interested in languages, this may be a great course for you. Be assured that no matter where you live, you'll never be the only Jew in a Hebrew language classroom.

- *Torah and Talmud:* Thousands of years of Jewish wisdom can be at your fingertips if you decide to look into these classes. Whether you're looking to strengthen your knowledge of Judaism or learn ways to improve your life, studying the Jewish texts can be a wonderful first step. Classes are available at Jewish Community Centers and synagogues all across America.

- *Kabbalah:* Kabbalah is all the rage nowadays and the Orthodox community is up in arms. According to Jewish tradition, only men who are well versed in the Torah and Talmud can study the Kabbalah. Unless you're Orthodox or particularly sensitive to their objections, don't worry about the detractors. Check if there's a Kabbalah centre, or some variation on the Kabbalah school theme, in your area and attend some free introductory classes to find out if this is the course for you.

- *Jewish history and culture:* Just because religion and spirituality don't strike any chords with you doesn't mean you can't use the academic approach to meet a nice Jewish boy and continue the 3,500-year legacy. Read literary works by great Jewish writers, study the origins of the Chosen People, or learn the meanings of different Jewish holidays and traditions. Whatever class you take, you're likely to encounter SJMs who share your interests. No matter what happens, however, you're sure to come out the wiser for the experience.

## JEWTOPIAS:
## JEWISH CAPITALS OF THE UNITED STATES

*Growing up in Omaha, Nebraska, I didn't meet too many Jewish guys. Both of the boyfriends I had in high school were Christian. When I got to college at the University of Nebraska, I wanted to meet more Jews and started going to the Hillel. I became pretty involved with the Jewish student life on campus. After graduation, I couldn't imagine moving back to Omaha. It's not that there aren't any Jews there, but the pickings are slim and I wanted to go somewhere with a more vibrant Jewish community. Like many of my non-Jewish friends, I picked Chicago because it's a bigger city, there's more professional opportunity, and it's still pretty close to my family in Nebraska. Best of all, I have met a lot of Jewish people and have no problem keeping my dating life kosher.*

—Gabi, twenty-four, Chicago

Living in Nebraska, a state with only three thousand or so Jews to its name, Gabi always felt strongly about her Jewish identity. Growing up Jewish in Omaha taught her to empathize with Jews over the ages. While she didn't experience overt anti-Semitism, she came of age feeling different, like an outsider, someone who didn't fit in. Since her chances of meeting and falling in love with one of the handful of Jewish Nebraskans were slim to none and she was unwilling to sacrifice her heritage for the sake of marriage, Gabi had only two options: Either fall in love with a non-Jew who was open to conversion or move to a city densely populated with other Jews.

For Gabi, Chicago proved to be a wise choice—not surprising considering the city boasts a Jewish population of 248,000, the fifth highest in the United States. Of the nearly six million Jews who call the United States home, about four million reside in one of eight metropolitan areas. When all is said and done, if you come from a goishe region, making the move to one of the following Jewtopias should exponentially increase your chances of winding up with an SJM—whether or not you ever set foot in a shul or a Jewish Community Center.

- *New York City:* About 9 percent of New York State's population is Jewish. Most of New York's Jews reside in and around New York City, the Jewish capital of the world. Just consider: The city has 1,256 synagogues, compared to 1,766 Protestant churches and 437 Roman Catholic churches. The tri-state region, which includes Connecticut and New Jersey, adds even more numbers to the 1.75 million Jews who live in the New York metropolitan area. All in all, this vicinity is home to approximately one-third of our country's Jews. No wonder most SJFs call it the promised land. *Main drawback:* From rent to the corner grocer, the cost of living doesn't get much higher.

- *Miami:* Coming in a distant second to New York City, the greater Miami area has 535,000 Jewish residents. While many of these Jews are in Miami only to enjoy their retirement, many others are young SJMs looking for someone just like you. *Main drawback:* Too many wannabe models and not enough brain surgeons.

• *Los Angeles:* Although Los Angeles is a widely spread out city, the fact that it's home to 490,000 Jews ensures that you won't be starving for Jewish humor for long. To hear current and former residents tell it, most of the stereotypes about the people being phony and materialistic also don't hold true across the board. *Main drawback:* No one ever claimed that the stereotypes are entirely unfounded.

• *Philadelphia:* What happens when you combine a city of 254,000 Jews with a relatively limited nightlife? High concentrations of single Jews intermingling. What more can an SJF and SJM ask for? *Main drawback:* If you're looking for a metropolis, you may be disappointed by Philadelphia's less-than-massive dimensions.

• *Chicago:* Chicago is the ideal location for anyone who wants all the big-city perks without the big-city attitude. Weighing in at a respectable 248,000 Jews, this is the only Midwestern city on the Jewtopia list. *Main drawback:* They don't call it the windy city for nothing. Brrr . . . it's cold.

• *San Francisco:* The ocean, the mountains, the architecture, the ingenious city planning, the 210,000 Jews . . . San Francisco is possibly one of the most idyllic cities in all of the United States. *Main drawback:* You get what you pay for—and in San Fran, you pay a lot.

• *Boston:* If you don't mind cold winters and have a thing for buildings that have been around since before the Declaration of Independence and the cobblestone streets that surround them, this little gem of a city features about 208,000 Jews for you to choose from. *Main drawback:* Get used to those layers; Boston winters can be long.

• *Washington, D.C.:* Surprise, surprise . . . another Jewish

# GREAT PLACES TO VISIT

Despite some ugly rumors to the contrary, we SJFs don't spend all our days in the pursuit of designer clothes, good restaurants, and the perfect manicure. As busy women, we work full-time jobs, make time for our families, and devote countless hours to maintaining our friendships. Often, there just isn't enough time in the day to meet a Jewish guy. That's where vacations come into the picture. With nothing to do but relax and enjoy, we can make the most of our time off by choosing our destinations wisely. The following locales are riddled with Jewish men:

- **Israel:** You'll have to go out of your way to avoid Jewish men in the Promised Land. If you're between the ages of eighteen and twenty-six, you can even take your trip for free. Birthright Israel offers ten-day jaunts to the land of milk and Jewish honeys free of charge to Jews who fall within this age group and have never been on an educational peer trip to Israel. Check them out on www.birthrightisrael.com. Unless you consider action-packed agendas a drawback, there is no catch. Enjoy it while you can. If you've missed the boat for Birthright Israel, consider taking some time out to work on a kibbutz.

- **Any Jewtopia:** Fortunately, every city on the Jewtopia list also doubles as a great vacation destination. You can easily spend a week or more in either New York, Miami, Los Angeles, or San Francisco without getting bored, while places like Chicago, Washington, D.C., Boston, and Philly are ideal for those long holiday weekends.

- **UJA Singles Missions:** Besides being a great place to volunteer and get involved with the Jewish community, the United Jewish Appeal also sponsors many trips for Jewish singles. On these missions, large groups of young Jewish singles go everywhere from eastern Europe to South America to Israel. With plenty of opportunity to learn about different cultures and each other, attendees often walk away from these trips with new friends and relationships.

• **The Hamptons (Southampton, Bridge Hampton, East Hampton, etc.):** Not just for New Yorkers, but for Jews all over the Northeast, Hamptons season begins on Memorial Day weekend and ends on Labor Day weekend. Come springtime, sharehouse organizers start advertising the availability of spots in the multibedroom homes they've rented for the summer. Depending on what kind of financial/time investments you're willing to make, you can buy a quarter share, which entitles you to four weekends of the summer, a half share, which gives you eight weekends, or you can go every weekend with a full share. With fifteen to thirty people staying in each house every weekend, you're certain to meet plenty of single Jews and potential love interests.

• **Abroad:** If you go in for international travel, then don't waste your time on the Spanish and Greek isles. These countries don't have twenty thousand Jews between them. When you're looking to mix age-old culture with young Jewish men, you're more likely to succeed in the following world capitals:

| City | Jewish Population |
| --- | --- |
| Paris | 350,000 |
| London | 200,000 |
| Moscow | 200,000 |
| Buenos Aires | 180,000 |
| Toronto | 175,000 |

capital on the Eastern Seaboard. Since this one also happens to be the national capital, brush up on your C-SPAN and get in touch with your social consciousness because word on the street has it that politics is all anyone wants to talk about inside the Beltway. If you'd rather talk religion, you'll be able to speak freely with about 165,000 Jews. *Main drawback:* Not for the apolitical.

## THE LAST WORD

Whether you have plenty of time to devote to the pursuit of an SJM or have only a few measly hours at your disposal, implementing the tips in this chapter should get you on your way. If you have your heart set on winding up with a Jew, you have to embrace this personal need as readily as you do the need for sleep, food, and shelter.

Holding out for what you want is always a challenge that requires a great deal of time and effort. To keep from losing hope and bending your own rules, you must become proactive. You may even have to slightly modify a few of your activities. For instance, if you're a yoga fanatic, you may consider making the switch from your regular studio to the one at the local JCC. In certain cases, you may even have to go thousands of miles out of your way—especially if your hometown has only a few single Jewish guys to go around.

Luckily, today's Jewish singles have no shortage of ways to augment their dating options. With the hopping Internet dating scene, the many Jewish singles trips, and services like SpeedDating, you need never be at a loss for companionship. In this day and age, the only thing standing between an SJF and a thriving relationship is her attitude. The more open you are to the possibilities, the more people will come into your life. The more people come into your life, the more likely you are to meet one who touches your heart. As it turns out, love, like the Torah, all comes down to numbers.

# chapter three

## Divided We Stand

*I dated one guy who was way more religious than me. He had spent a lot of time in Israel, went by his Hebrew name (which drove me crazy for some reason) and was all-around more religious than I was. It was a little uncomfortable for me because I grew up in such a Reform community. I felt like as the relationship progressed my religious indifference would have caused a lot of tension. I don't want religion to be a part of my relationship and with him it was always there. I don't need to be constantly reminded of my religion, I know what I am.*

—Beth, thirty, Shaker Heights, Ohio

Each of us relates to Judaism in our own special way. Some of us bestow a great deal of weight upon the heritage, dating Jewish, peppering sentences with Yiddishisms like *meshugas*, reading Jewish newspapers, and joining every Jewish organization in the vicinity. But that's not even half the story. The fact is that most of us relegate Judaism to a footnote on our CVs and grow perplexed at the mere thought of dating anyone "more Jewish" than ourselves.

To further complicate matters, Judaism is not always so conveniently broken down into "more Jewish" or "less Jewish" categories. Instead, what we have is a variety of different movements, and each takes a unique and varied position on what it means to be a proper Jew. First, you've got your three main branches: Orthodox, Conservative, and Reform. Then, you've got your variations: Modern Orthodox and Conservadox. Throw in the relatively new Reconstructionists, and you've got enough denominations to make your head spin. Unfortunately, you'd still be leaving out about 50 percent of us Jews who call ourselves "traditional," "unaffiliated," "secular," "lapsed," "non-practicing," or just plain "hostile."

Just take a look at JDate. While the site is for only Jewish singles, there is a religion category that asks you to identify yourself and the SJM of your dreams as any of the following:

- Orthodox (Ba'al Teshuva)
- Conservative
- Conservadox
- Hassidic
- Modern Orthodox
- Orthodox (Frum)
- Reconstructionist
- Reform
- Secular
- Traditional
- Unaffiliated
- Another Stream

The recent flap over interdenominational dating is a case in point. In the summer of 2003, a pair of Orthodox Jewish grad students issued a widely discussed pamphlet accusing the Hillel organization (a foundation promoting Jewish community on college campuses) of promoting dating among different Jewish streams, thereby endangering the integrity of Orthodox students.

Not to be outdone, Reform and unaffiliated Jews, like Beth from Shaker Heights, have their own litany of complaints when it comes to dating SJMs who are fairly religious. Issues such as keeping kosher, going to synagogue, and observing Shabbat can come between couples from varying points on the Jewish observance spectrum. Many SJFs who are looking to meet their male equivalent either underestimate or overestimate what different degrees of piety can mean to a relationship down the line.

Before you let a little thing like a *kippah* stand in the way of a potentially beautiful friendship, you may want to learn more about:

- The fundamentals of various Jewish denominations and perspectives.

- Facing the challenges of dating a nonpracticing Jew.

- Where you stand on the religious issue.

- The role of communication in bridging religious gaps.

- How to negotiate a mutually satisfying interdenominational relationship.

## JEWISH STREAMS: WHAT'S THE DIFFERENCE?

*I met Ben at a nightclub. He worked in banking and was completing a novel on the side. I thought he was cute, well-rounded, funny, and stable, so we started hanging out. Everything seemed normal at first, except he didn't like to go out to eat. I was beginning to wonder; but then he confessed to me that he was Modern Orthodox and kept kosher. He was also very active in the Jewish community and had not had sex since he became Orthodox. Fortunately, he made an exception for me, or we would not have lasted a month. In the end, I don't think we were compatible. And I'm not sure if I could have tolerated his devotion to religion, considering I'm what his people would call a "bad" Jew.*

—Candice, twenty-seven, San Diego

Candice's experience is far from uncommon. Many of us have very little idea of what the different Jewish denominations represent, much less how they relate to dating. In this section, you'll discover what you can expect when you're going out with someone who comes from a different sect of Judaism. Remember, there are no hard-and-fast rules. Even Orthodox Jews have been known to cave to the occasional Big Mac attack, sneaking into the decidedly not kosher confines of McDonald's for an illicit taste of those famous all-beef patties. Meanwhile, there is an entire cross-section of Jews who try to keep kosher as best they can even while they consider themselves unaffiliated with any organized stream of Judaism. Go figure.

The following are the four main branches of Judaism and what you can expect when dating their adherents.

## ORTHODOX

Considered the most authentic, legitimate, and demanding of all the Jewish streams, Orthodox Judaism is an umbrella term for a number of slightly divergent yet highly proud groups. Whatever their differences and pecking order, every Orthodox set believes that God gave the Torah and Talmud to Moses on Mount Sinai. Accordingly, Orthodox Jews (who make up about 10 percent of the U.S. Jewish population) believe in the literal translation of the Torah. That every word has special meaning, and every single one of the 613 commandments must be observed, regardless of financial hardship, personal feelings, or convenience.

Your experience with Orthodox men will probably be limited to the Modern Orthodox, who differ from the traditional Orthodox only in their choice of dress (no black suits and fedoras here) and willingness to consort with the less observant. Modern Orthodox guys may not refuse to shake your hand for fear of impure thoughts, but they will most likely:

- Put off having premarital sex until they are sure of you and their feelings.

- Keep kosher.

- Observe Shabbat.

- Celebrate all the Jewish holidays (even those you've never heard of).

- Take an active role in their synagogue and Jewish community.

- Not consider remarriage without a *get* (a Jewish divorce document).

- Not accept you as a Jew if you're "Jewish on your father's side" (even if your mother underwent a Reform conversion, which doesn't hold water according to Orthodox rules).

If you veer toward the secular and fancy yourself a free-thinker, be prepared to deal with much angst on the part of your Modern Orthodox paramour and don't be surprised if a lot of otherwise rational debates end with the words "It's right there in Leviticus." Here is what one Jewish woman had to say about being the wife of a Modern Orthodox Jew: "I find it very difficult being married to an Orthodox Jew, being an atheist myself. The rules he follows are very restrictive, especially on holidays and Sabbaths. When we were dating, we did not spend these times together."

Then again, you may find the stability of a structured lifestyle comforting, like Sara, a twenty-nine-year-old sales rep from Merrick, New York:

> *I loved that he had this family tradition behind him. It made me feel comfortable and emotionally secure to know there was a way of life that he followed. Like a structure that he'd never break. Every Friday at the house we'd have all the lights off and wouldn't take calls. I liked the predictability of it. My only problem was that he was reluctant to have sex until we got to know each other better. I thought we knew each other well enough long before he was ready.*

## CONSERVATIVE

The common misconception that Conservative is the same as Reform is due mostly to a laxity on the part of certain Conservative Jews. In reality, the Conservative movement is more in keeping with the Orthodox than with the more liberal Reform denomination. Ostensibly, Conservative Jews are also bound to keep kosher and do as the Orthodox, it is in spirit that they differ. The paradox of the Conservatives' viewpoint lies in their belief that while God gave us the Torah and Talmud, there is also a significant human component to these sacred texts.

If you happen to run across a staunch Conservative, you can expect them to follow the same rules as the Orthodox—kosher, Shabbat, the works. Most Conservatives, however, pick and choose which rules to observe and which to circumvent. For instance, they may:

- Follow variations on the kosher theme, keeping kosher only in the home or restricting their observance of dietary guidelines to abstaining from pork and shellfish.

- Flout the laws of sexual conduct and not hesitate to succumb to your feminine wiles.

- Insist on attending Saturday morning services, but drive, use the phone, and engage in other forbidden behaviors.

Typically, Conservative Jews and Reform Jews can co-exist peacefully within the bounds of a romantic relationship. Sometimes, theoretical disagreements may crop up. Although Conservatives believe in adhering to Jewish law, they bend the rules with wanton abandon and can sometimes be mistaken for hypocrites. For example, you may wonder why they refuse to eat lobster, but chow down on cheeseburgers. Or you may get annoyed that they insist on going to Saturday morning services when they don't bother to light Shabbat candles on Friday nights. In the end, you'll have to resign yourself to the possibility that Conservatives are more concerned with preserving Jewish laws than heeding them.

Veronica, a twenty-four-year-old from Boca Raton, Florida, had this experience:

> I dated a pretty religious Conservative for about a year. He would not use the phone during Shabbat or turn on the lights. So every Friday night, we had to be together. I would sleep over and stay all of Saturday. Since he couldn't drive on Saturdays either, I had to drive us everywhere, including the synagogue. Also, he'd watch TV only if I turned it on. Stuff like that. It made no sense to me. But whenever I'd ask him about it, he'd say that it didn't matter what I did because I wasn't going to keep Shabbat anyway.

Of course, the experience can also be a positive one, as Rob, thirty-four from Washington, D.C., found out:

*Right from the beginning, I was impressed by Alissa's self-assurance and values. As I found out, a lot of these qualities came from her stong belief in Judaism. I was a struggling artist, smoking a lot of pot, and living a crazy life when I met Alissa. Even though I was annoyed that she kept kosher and refused to eat anything but salad at my favorite restaurants, she helped bring me down to earth. It took a few years before we were both ready, but now we're married and parents, and I'm satisfied with the decision I made.*

## REFORM

The Reform movement sees God not as the author of the Torah and Talmud, but as the inspiration of the writers who were also influenced by the norms and mores of their times. As a result, the Reform movement gives great weight to individual freedom. Reform Jews act as autonomous beings, making up their own minds as to which rituals and traditions they will follow.

Practically speaking, most Reform Jews are of the Big Three variety. The "Big Three" being:

- Observing the High Holidays (Rosh Hashanah and Yom Kippur).

- Lighting the menorah on Hanukkah.

- Attending a seder on Passover.

As to what all this means in terms of dating, that depends on your own position. If you are nonreligious, as in secular or lapsed, you may enjoy being with someone who is grounded in the Jewish tradition without being overbearing. If, on the other hand, you are more religious, you may find yourself resenting your Reform Jewish boyfriend's relaxed attitudes. When twenty-seven-year-old

Tamar first got involved with her current boyfriend, she was Orthodox, he wasn't. Here is her take on what happened:

> When we started dating, I was more religious, and it was tough. He became more religious for me for a while, which was hard on him. And all the while it was hard for me to see him as less religious because it made me judgmental. Thankfully, I became secular and since then we've both been much happier.

## RECONSTUCTIONIST

Since there are only about 250,000 Reconstructionist Jews in the United States (as opposed to 1.25 million Reform, 1.25 million Conservative, and 600,000 Orthodox), don't feel too bad if this is the first time you're hearing about this stream. The Reconstructionists take Judaism as seriously as the most devoted members of the Orthodox and Conservative camps, but that's where the similarities end.

Reconstructionism sees Judaism as an ever-evolving religion and culture that's in step with humanity's progress over the millennia, not as a set of rules handed down by God to be kept sacred and followed blindly for all eternity. The Reconstructionist credo is, "The past has a vote, not a veto." This denomination's idea of God also diverges from the more traditional groups. Namely, they see God not as a supreme being hovering over our affairs from the heavens, but as the force of goodness that lies within each of us.

If you're dating a Reconstructionist Jew, don't expect him to keep kosher or follow any specific guidelines. His Judaism will probably be a very personal expression of faith and pride in his heritage. Reconstructionists don't care whether it's your mother or your father who's Jewish. As long as you have one Jewish parent and you think you're Jewish, you're in the club. No doubt, this is one reason the more stringent Jewish factions refer to Reconstructionism as "touchy-feely" Judaism. If you're a touchy-feely person who enjoys the warm and fuzzy approach, Reconstructionist SJMs may be just the ticket.

## SHOW ME THE REASON: THE THREE FACES OF A SECULAR JEW

*I'm not super religious, but I do believe that Judaism is more than a culture. It's a religion. If I call myself a Jew, I have to accept certain responsibilities. Such as going to shul for Shabbat, giving tzedakah, taking part in the Jewish community, and ultimately, marrying a Jewish man and raising Jewish children. I'm sorry, but I just don't understand how someone can go around saying they're Jewish without doing any of these things.*

—Melissa, thirty-one, St. Louis, Missouri

With more than 50 percent of all U.S. Jews calling themselves nonpracticing, spiritual, universalist, humanistic, agnostic, atheist, or Zen Buddhist, SJFs who share Melissa's viewpoint are in the minority. If you're going to be dating SJMs whom you meet outside the walls of a synagogue, you'll need to be prepared for a variety of attitudes relating to Judaism.

Although secular Jews differ in their ideological underpinnings, most fall into one of the following three categories:

### GEFILTE FISH JEWS (AKA CULTURED JEWS)

*General attitude:* "You're getting married? *Mazel tov!* I'll drink to that . . . L'chaim!" A cultured Jew's emphasis on Judaism does not extend far beyond humorous and numerous admissions of Jewish guilt. Do not mistake these stabs at Jewish humor for piety. Cultured Jews are proud to be Jewish, but mostly because Jews make up a disproportionately large percentage of Nobel Prize laureates, Adam Sandler wrote a funny song about Hanukkah, and *Seinfeld* is one of the most popular shows in TV history.

In most cases, such an SJM has only a superficial connection to the religion. If he wants to settle down with an SJF, it's probably for the sake of his parents or because he enjoys the free and uncensored exchange of Jewish jokes. From time to time, you may run across the rare cultured Jew who has a genuine appreciation for Judaism's many contributions to modern civilization. His interest in Judaism, however, is more a testament to his intellectual curiosity than a feeling of belonging and unity with the Jewish people. *Dating advice:* Cultured Jews shouldn't pose a problem for SJFs who don't take the whole "Jewish thing" very seriously.

## BAGEL JEWS (AKA ASSIMILATED JEWS)

*General attitude:* "I suppose you could say that I'm Jewish. But I prefer to think of myself as American." If you attempt Jewish bonding here, you'll be barking up the wrong tree. Like the bagel, these Jews are so thoroughly assimilated into U.S. culture, the fact that they're Jewish is basically immaterial. Bagel Jews don't focus too much on their own Judaism or anybody else's. Some have Christmas trees while others chant and meditate before little sculptures of Buddha.

For most assimilated Jews, anti-Semitism and religious persecution are things of the past. We've come a long way from those dark days when being Jewish meant you were "different." We're all human, all in the same boat, all similar and different at the same time. *Dating Advice:* Assimilated Jews have many solid reasons for not giving more weight to their Jewish roots, so don't try to awaken their inner Jew unless you want to butt heads.

*My mother is Jewish and my father is not. I know that to some people this makes me a Jew, but not to me. I grew up in Kentucky, with no religious feelings whatsoever. My girlfriend is Presbyterian and I don't believe in God. Once in a while, I'll meet someone ridiculous enough to tell me that I'm in denial about my identity. But if they think I'm a self-hating Jew or that I should be dating Jewish or following some Jewish traditions just because my mother is Jewish, that's their problem. I just do what I believe is right for me.*

*—James, thirty-two, Louisville, Kentucky*

## BACON JEWS (AKA HOSTILE JEWS)

*General attitude:* "Jewish girls are JAPs and the guys who put them on pedestals are chumps." We all harbor stereotypes that we've picked up on our journey through life, but bacon Jews truly fancy themselves experts based on what they perceive to be their extensive experience with other Jews. This group can be categorized as hostile, since many such SJMs would never even give an SJF a chance because they are convinced that every Jewish woman is a whiny, materialistic, high-maintenance snob who spends her days shopping and her nights eating take-out while emasculating her boyfriend.

*In my most radical identity–politics phase in college, I realized that if you could not love another Jew, you could not love the Jew in yourself and were just acting out self-hatred. I feel this is particularly true of Jewish men. If they can't accept a woman who is and behaves "Jewish," it's probably because they feel alienated from their Jewishness and from society and are seeking the acceptance of non-Jewish society by dating a non-Jewish girl.*

*—Ilana, twenty-five, Santa Monica, California*

The immaturity inherent in such narrow perspectives should be enough of a deterrent to most SJFs. But beware, many hostile Jews will not risk the censure that comes of revealing their shocking opinions too soon. They'll wait until they get to know a woman better before unveiling their inner self-hating Jew. *Dating advice:* To be fair, for every such SJM, there is an equally hostile SJF who thinks Jewish guys are all wimpy Mama's boys who couldn't possibly have anything to offer a real woman. When these two meet, the mutual hostility cancels each other out and romance is imminent. All other SJFs should take the advice of Marlene from New Jersey: "Jewish men who will not date Jewish women are the type to be avoided. They think way too much of themselves, and they stereotype too easily."

## CAN'T WE ALL JUST GET ALONG?

Unless you're part of an Orthodox sect, as sure of life's dos and don'ts as you are of the letters in the Hebrew alphabet, then you may need to give some thought to how you relate to Jews with a different slant on their identity.

The following quiz is designed to give you an idea of how skilled you'll be at dating a Jew who is either more or less Jewish than you.

1. Your beliefs are most closely aligned with which perspective?

   a. Conservadox
   b. Conservative
   c. Reform or Reconstuctionist
   d. Non-practicing

**2.** How certain are you that your belief system is accurate and true?

   a. 100% . . . Those who disagree aren't stupid, they just haven't seen the light.
   b. 75% . . . I allow for different opinions, but deep down, I'm pretty sure I'm right.
   c. 50% . . . It's not about certainty, it's about what works best for me.
   d. 25% . . . I don't know what to believe. I'm still looking for answers.

**3.** How important is it that your closest friends have the same religious beliefs and/or philosophy of life?

   a. It doesn't matter. As long as they're good people and we connect on other levels, I say live and let live.
   b. Very important. How else will they understand and relate to my experience?
   c. I don't care about that. My personal beliefs are still up for negotiation. As long as we like to do the same things, I'm happy.
   d. It's nice when they do, but not a dealbreaker. As long as they have good reasons for their beliefs, I'm more than happy to learn from different opinions.

**4.** How would you react if you made plans to go on a dinner date and found out that your companion either keeps kosher, can't go out on a Friday night because he keeps Shabbat, or is in some way more observant than your are?

   a. I would accept it for the time being, but it would bring up some serious doubts as to the future of our relationship.
   b. I would cancel plans. Why even bother getting involved with someone so different?
   c. If there is good chemistry, I'd bring the issue into the open. I don't mind if someone is more religious and I'd want to find out if he is okay with me being less religious.
   d. I'd be happy. Maybe he would be a good influence.

**5.** If you and a good friend or significant other disagree on a pivotal issue, how do you resolve the problem?

    a. I argue until he or she sees it my way.

    b. I agree to disagree. If my friend can't deal with that, it's his problem.

    c. I usually cave and let her think she's won the argument.

    d. I strike a compromise so we can move on and not get stuck on the same problem again in the future.

**6.** If your identity were a movie, what role would you give to Judaism?

    a. Leading role. I'm very aware of being Jewish. In fact, it's right up there with female, daughter, and Zionist in terms of things that define me as a person.

    b. Bit part. Maybe I'll think about it more later, but I haven't put any undue stress on it up to now and I'm still doing all right.

    c. Supporting player. I love the heritage and am proud of my roots, but there's a lot more to me and to life than that.

    d. An extra left on the cutting room floor. I don't see how being Jewish has anything to do with who I am as a person.

**7.** Can you see yourself settling down with an SJM who has a different take on Judaism?

    a. Never! What would my children/parents/friends think?

    b. Of course. A Jew is a Jew.

    c. Only if he was more observant. I need someone to inspire me.

    d. Only if he was less observant. I don't feel bound to ritual.

**8.** If you had to pick one of the following to describe your group of friends, which would you choose?

    a. Homogenous . . . All Jewish, all with more or less the same degree of piety, or lack thereof.

b. Eclectic . . . Most of us are Jewish, but not all of us, and everyone has different ideas.

c. Diverse . . . We come from all walks of life and are connected by the compatibility of our personalities.

d. Fragmented . . . I don't have one group of friends. I move among groups, making individual connections.

9. If you believe in God, how would you react if you were on a date with someone who didn't believe in any power higher than nature. Or if you don't believe in God, how would you react if you were out with someone who did?

a. I would take him out of the running immediately, tune out, and spend the rest of the night pushing back my cuticles.

b. I would reserve judgment until I got to know him better.

c. It would be a big minus, but I wouldn't discount him just for that.

d. I wouldn't care. He will come to see things my way . . . eventually.

10. When you think of someone who is more or less observant than yourself, you think:

a. He may judge me unfavorably and have a hard time understanding my point of view.

b. Ten minutes with me and he'll be all turned around.

c. Great. I finally get to meet someone with a different perspective.

d. He is self-righteous, closed-minded, and/or deluded.

## SCORING
Give yourself the following points for each answer and then add the points together for a total score.

1. a = 1, b = 2, c = 3, d = 2      4. a = 1, b = 0, c = 3, d = 2
2. a = 0, b = 1, c = 3, d = 2      5. a = 0, b = 2, c = 1, d = 3
3. a = 3, b = 0, c = 1, d = 2      6. a = 1, b = 2, c = 3, d = 1

**7.** a = 0, b = 3, c = 1, d = 1       **9.** a = 0, b = 3, c = 2, d = 1
**8.** a = 0, b = 1, c = 2, d = 3      **10.** a = 2, b = 1, c = 3, d = 0

## RESULTS

● **24 and over = Easygoing:** You are an open-minded pluralist and should have little to no trouble getting along with someone either more or less religious than you are. If you hear that your date can eat out only at a Kosher restaurant, you're game. Why not try something different, you figure. As for keeping Shabbat, it's a small price to pay for true love. Just remember, seeking new experiences is all well and good as long as you know what your comfort zone is. Sometimes going along to get along can go on for too long. Make sure you're not putting your personal feelings and beliefs aside just to please others.

● **14-23 = Middle of the Road:** You're secure in your beliefs, but not entirely closed off to other ways of thinking. You can listen to conflicting perspectives without getting defensive and flying off the handle. You've even been known to change your mind from time to time. Despite all this, developing a relationship with an SJM who doesn't share your point of view should pose a challenge. Chances are that you will gravitate toward someone who is on the same page. If, by some strange twist of fate, chemistry should steer you in the direction of someone whose ideas clash with your own, compromise and open communication will be crucial for your relationship to survive.

● **13 or less = Set in Your Ways:** If you're observant, forget about trying to put up with an SJM who likes to spend his Saturday mornings sleeping in. If he doesn't start dragging his sorry *tuchis* out of bed and into shul, he'll be one sorry slacker. If you're on the nonpracticing side of the divide, your Kosher-loving honey will just have to grin and bear the sight of you noshing on eggs Benedict (Canadian bacon and all) at brunch—whether he likes it or not. In fact, you may even try to tempt him into taking a bite. Unless you open your mind to other viewpoints, you'll need to stick with your own kind.

## CAN WE TALK:
## COMMUNICATION IS THE ANSWER

*Looking back, I would have made it clear, before marriage, that I would bring the kids up according to my Judaism, and not my husband's and that I would expect him to give as much priority to it, for their sake, as I did. Instead, I kind of let things slide, so my kids don't feel it as much as I do.*

—Marlene, forty-eight, Paramus, New Jersey

Once you get past the initial shock of finding yourself attracted to an unlike-minded Jew, you may begin to consider the possibility of taking this person seriously. "If I overlook this one major flaw," you tell yourself, "he actually makes for pretty good boyfriend/husband/father material." Sometimes, you're not nearly so practical. Instead, the feelings are so intense, they cloud your judgment. "So what if he's Orthodox," you think, "true love does not discriminate."

In the first few weeks, even months, of an interdenominational romance, you're likely to take one of two positions:

- We're not compatible. I can't take this relationship seriously.

- We're in love. We'll make it work despite our religious differences.

Don't get attached to either attitude, because the chances of it outlasting the early phases of your relationship are slim. Despite your best intentions to the contrary, you may develop feelings for someone with a different take on Judaism and wind up having to face your incompatibilities. Or, if you fall headlong and overlook the differences early on, you may find that compromising is more of a challenge than you anticipated.

To make sure that your new relationship represents a healthy balance between your beliefs and those of your SJM, follow these guidelines from the very beginning.

## GET INTO HIS HEAD

Before you can accept another perspective, you have to try to understand it. Ask yourself, do you know what role being Jewish plays in your SJM's life? Which of his needs are fulfilled by religion? How does his perspective of Judaism benefit his life? Is it order he craves? Spirituality? Both?

We all tend to assume that others understand us . . . especially if they don't ask follow-up questions. So fire away. If he does something you consider silly or nonsensical, ask him his reasons. The rationales may surprise you. Once you wrap your brain around the full complexity and implications of his positions, you will be able to be more compassionate and accepting of his perspective, even if it does not match your own. Either that, or you'll decide that he's a complete lobotomy case and go on your merry way.

## BE YOUR OWN ADVOCATE

Getting into another person's head is crucial to increasing intimacy and forging a bond, but it will all be for naught if you lose yourself in the process. Remember the Jewish saying "If I am not for myself, who will be for me?" and never get so caught up in your significant other's experience that you forget about your own. Your feelings and beliefs are equally important.

Sometimes, the struggle to be understood is even more difficult than the struggle to understand. Especially since as women, we tend to want to nurture and cater to the men in our lives. Consequently, we often let them off the hook far too easily. "Sometimes men need to be humored and babied," we say, implying that men are somehow not as smart as we are and denying ourselves the mutual understanding that is the hallmark of any great relationship.

Being your own advocate involves fighting for your rights. As easy as it is to give in and abnegate our responsibility to ourselves, we must demand that our partners accept and respect our wishes and feelings as much as we do theirs if we are to thrive within our interdenominational romances.

> Joel and I had been together for nearly a year when we got engaged. When I met him, he was Modern Orthodox and I was not observant. During our relationship, he was the breadwinner and provider. I think he thought he could control me with his buying power. And maybe he was right. I made many sacrifices for him. I wore long skirts and long sleeves. I observed Shabbat and kept Kosher. I thought I did it because I loved him. Eventually, I faced up to the fact that I was doing all the compromising in the relationship because I was financially dependent on him. I ended our engagement and I am back to being secular. He still tries to call, offering to give me the life I want. He promises vacations, dinners, nights at the theater, but I'm a different person now.
>
> —Jodi, thirty-three, New York

## PICK YOUR BATTLES

We all know people who let others walk all over them. No one knows where they stand because like doormats, they're always lying down. That's one extreme. On the opposite end are those people who are so vigilant and defensive that everyone around them feels as if they were living in a minefield. One wrong step and—bam!—you're in the middle of a blowout. The least disagreement can turn into an all-out war when you're overzealous in representing your best interests.

Keep in mind that reciprocity is the key to give and take. Pay attention not only to your own sacrifices, but to the ones your partner is making for you. (For instance, is he skipping out on Friday night services early to be with you? Is he staying away from pork out of deference to your beliefs?) Armed with this well-rounded perspective, you'll know exactly when you're doing too much and when you're not doing enough as well as when to stand up for yourself and when to hold your tongue.

## HAVE THE COURAGE OF YOUR CONVICTIONS

In this day and age, we pay a lot of lip service to honesty, courage, and strength of character, but when it comes to relationships these values often go spiraling down the nearest drainpipe. Instead, many of us give in to fear. Afraid to express our honest feelings and beliefs lest we scare off a perfectly good guy, we stay mum on the very topics that need our attention the most.

To be sure, open communication is easier in theory than in practice. How many times have you wanted to say, "I hate that you don't call when you say you will" but instead decided to play the "I don't care" game by not picking up the phone when the gentleman caller finally materialized? When he does it again and again, you wonder . . . what's his problem? Doesn't this guy get it? Can't he read my mind? Isn't it obvious? That's the flaw in being passive aggressive. If you never muster the courage to tell him what you really want—be that more reliable phone calls or a Hebrew school education for your babies—you can never complain when you don't get it.

Instead of tailoring our wish list to that of our significant other just to avoid rocking the boat or keeping the relationship strictly casual because we're afraid of how religious differences will affect our relationship down the line, we need to bring our personal feelings and all related concerns out into the open. If the only reason you can't see yourself settling down with your boyfriend is because he is Modern Orthodox and you're Reform, tell him that you need to talk and express yourself over dinner or drinks.

No doubt, you'll need to work together to achieve a balance. Compromise involves two parties making concessions, not one person doing all the work and feeling resentful while the other sits around taking it all for granted. Make sure that you and your partner are both putting in your fair share with a simple system of checks and balances: If one of you does something offensive, make sure the other speaks up. That way, when and if he does it again, you'll know that he's not clueless but inconsiderate and quite possibly not right for you.

## AVOID THE MISSIONARY POSITION

Leave the missionary work to Mother Teresa's disciples because there's no room for proselytizing in a relationship. There is a fine line between asking for what you want and trying to impose your belief system on your partner. Figure out if you can accept your SJM the way he is, whether he is more or less religious than you, and don't try to convert him to your way of thinking.

Of course, the laissez-faire approach is not nearly as simple as it seems. There will be countless times when you'll feel tempted to step in and give him an earful of your advice. No matter how much you want to share your personal philosophy on life, resist the urge to preach at all costs. Instead of finding your assistance helpful, your SJM will probably just see you as condescending, arrogant, and unsympathetic. If you truly believe that your way is best, then lead by example—if that doesn't persuade him, nothing will. In the end, you'll either learn to tolerate the differences or go your separate ways.

## THE LAST WORD

Tolerance, compassion, and acceptance are the cornerstones of every healthy relationship, but they're even more important when religious differences enter into the equation. Usually, we SJFs will keep to guys who share our views on what it means to be Jewish and never have reason to doubt our positions. It is only when we wander outside our comfort zones that we come up against our own limitations.

Some of us will decide that bridging the gap between two disparate worldviews is not in the cards. As countless SJFs and SJMs have testified in conversations with me, interdenominational romance is clearly not for everyone. Those of us who do choose to give it the old college try, if only for the sake of love, will have our work cut out for us right from the jump.

Before we can engage in a relationship of equals with an SJM who has a different approach to Judaism, we need to come to terms with our own take on the religion and appreciate that being Jewish means different things to different people. Only when we have a comprehensive understanding of our partner's beliefs and our own can we begin to figure out where the halfway point truly lies. For a more in-depth treatment of this complex topic check out the books listed in Aditional Resources on page 179.

# chapter four

## Nice Jewish Girls

*I hate dating. Especially getting fixed up. It's the worst when I don't like the guy, and he doesn't get it. He'll keep calling, and I have to make all kinds of excuses for why I can't see him. Sometimes, this goes on for so long, we'll actually get to be friends. Phone friends. I feel bad, but I don't want to hurt his feelings or upset the people who set us up. I think I'm just too nice. I have to become meaner.*

—Liz, twenty-three, New York

In today's world of cable-modem love connections, Hurry-Date, and fast-paced romance, many of us fly from one date to the next, forgetting names, confusing identifying information, and deleting phone numbers faster than we can say "It's not you, it's me." In our rush to find love, happiness, and "the one," we may begin to see dating as a numbers game and overlook one not-so-minor detail . . . the human element.

How many times have you conveniently forgotten to return a call? Or neglected to tell your date that you're still not over your ex? Even wrote a guy off just for his choice of footwear? We've all done it. Of course, frequent wrongs don't make a right. Not according to Judaism, which would have you consider how you would feel if someone left you hanging after repeated attempts at contact, misled you into thinking they were no longer attached to an ex-girlfriend, or decided that you weren't worth his time because your shoes were just a little *too* pointy.

As single Jewish females, we can use Judaism as a foundation for all our actions. Besides a religion, Judaism is an ethical framework, structured to minimize the pain and discomfort others may feel as a result of our actions. Karma, universal law, the Golden Rule . . . whatever you call it, it comes down to this: What goes around comes around, so as Rabbi Hillel said, "Do not do unto others as you would not have done unto you."

Sounds deceptively simple. But how does Hillel's dictum really relate to dating? Can it actually be that easy to know what is right in every circumstance? Take Liz, whose story launched this chapter. She thinks she's doing the right thing by making excuses to the guy pursuing her instead of telling him straight out that she's not interested. She figures that he'll eventually get tired of her behavior and stop calling on his own. That way, his feelings won't get hurt.

Meanwhile, her gentleman caller thinks that she'll eventually find the time for him. By not doing anything to disabuse him of this delusion, Liz is wasting his time and energy—not to mention her own. If she simply told him that she was not interested in anything more than his friendship, he could stop making excuses for her behavior, deal with the temporary discomfort, and get on with his life. Maybe that is what Liz meant when she said she needs to become "meaner," because this is certainly one case in which she needs to be cruel to be kind.

Hillel's motto is a catch-all phrase. When he said, "What is hateful to yourself do not do to your fellow-man. This is the entire Torah, the rest is commentary. Go and study" (Babylonian Talmud, *Shabbat* 31a), he was stating that the implications of his maxim are far-reaching and often counterintuitive. To avoid doing to others what you yourself would find hateful, you must first understand yourself—likes, dislikes, needs, fears, drives, insecurities, and so forth. Furthermore, you must be sufficiently compassionate to empathize with other people's feelings. Then, to top it all off, you'll need to take the time to relate and figure out how you would not want to be treated under similar circumstances.

Ethical living is a tall order, but no one ever said that being Jewish would be a piece of rugelach. Fact is, doing the wrong thing usually involves far less thought and effort than standing up for what is right. Unfortunately, wrongdoing never does give us any real sense of satisfaction, while taking the high road strengthens our characters, boosts our self-esteem, and ennobles our spirits. Best of all, acting with integrity begins to feel more natural with practice. If you've heard it once, you've heard it a million times: Short-term pain, long-term gain—and vice versa.

In this chapter, you'll find advice for the common ethical dating dilemmas that may stump you. You'll read about situations that involve:

- Proper etiquette.

- Playing hard to get.

- Different types of dishonesty.

- Rebound relationships.

- Constructive vs. destructive criticism.

- Breakups.

Even if you don't find the advice you seek in here, you can use the principles as guidelines for how to handle yourself in any situation.

## ETIQUETTE: NOT JUST FOR WASPS

*Sometimes, I just don't want to be hit on. I know it's not nice, but when guys come up to me and I'm not attracted, I'll give them the cold shoulder until they leave me alone.*

—Sara, twenty-two, Los Angeles

Many men sympathize with us women because we have to put up with guys who don't know how to behave themselves (that is, guys who lose the ability to distinguish the line between charming flirt and sexual harasser after just a few drinks). But men don't have a monopoly on bad behavior. As Sara said, "I know it's not nice, but . . . " Yes, we SJFs can also use a little compassion and sensitivity training when it comes to dealing with men.

Believe it or not, approaching a total stranger is no easier for a man than it is for a woman. No matter how confident we are in our ability to interest a member of the opposite sex, there is nothing like a swift rejection to send our egos into a free fall. After enough bad experiences, even the most balanced, together guy may decide that going out on the line is just not worth the trouble.

If like Sara, you've found yourself summarily dismissing perfectly nice guys whose only crime was to find you approachable, consider the following:

• The cute guy in the corner may not be coming up to you because he's afraid you'll be as rude as the last woman he tried speaking to . . . four months ago.

• If your brother or best male friend were in a bar getting dissed by a woman right now, how would you feel about her?

• What if you tried to talk to a guy, and he responded with some variation on the withering stare theme? Consider how you'd like to be treated under similar circumstances.

• This is a new person, you may learn something from a different perspective, make a new friend, or even develop an attraction. The worst that can happen is you'll exchange pleasantries and then excuse yourself.

Honestly, if you don't want to be approached by strangers, consider going out to dinner and a movie or just entertaining your friends at home. If you're going to be in a social setting, take personal responsibility for making the public venue a nice place to visit (and, no, that does not mean dancing on top of the bar). Here are a few techniques to implement when you're truly not interested:

• Be kind, consider how much courage it must have taken for Mr. Wrong to come up and talk to you.

• Mention a boyfriend (imaginary or otherwise) as soon as there's an opening, he'll get the point and won't take it personally.

• Don't waste his money and your time by letting him buy you a drink.

• Say "I'm going to find my friend/the bar/the ladies' room, it's been nice talking to you" and walk away.

• Go up to a guy you've never met before and strike up a conversation, just to see how the other half feels.

*If a guy calls or e-mails me, I always wait at least a day to respond. I don't want to seem too eager, plus I know the anticipation and uncertainty drive them crazy.*

—Mia, twenty-six, Chicago

Drive men crazy with your cool personality, your keen intelligence, your sparkling wit, your sweet disposition, even your new hairstyle, but whatever you do, stay away from cheap tricks like phone games. Unless your intention is to display your own lack of interest and make the guy feel unimportant, playing mind games with communication devices is ill-advised.

When you truly want to get to know someone better, act like it. Be responsible when returning phone calls and e-mails so that the guy gets a sense of where he stands with you. Put yourself in his shoes. Let's say you e-mailed a guy you like and didn't hear back from him that day? How would you feel? Probably, a bit anxious. Now, let's say you don't hear from him the next day . . . would it be fair to assume that you might be somewhat upset? By the time he finally got around to responding, you may very well have written him off all together. If you decided to go ahead and give him one last chance, he'd be skating on pretty thin ice. In any case, you are far less likely to either e-mail or call if you know he is irresponsible and too busy to be bothered by the likes of you.

If you make certain to treat men with respect, you will be in a position to demand the same consideration in return. On the other hand, when you consistently put off returning your calls and frequently bail out on plans, you forfeit the right to complain when someone does the same to you. Worse still, you'll never know whether the guy with whom you've been playing games is actually irresponsible and/or disinterested or whether he actually cares but is just retaliating in a passive-aggressive way.

Simply put, mind games are the end of mental clarity and a block to open communication. Isn't it hard enough to discern another person's feelings and intentions without throwing more wrenches into the works?

> *I've been known to give out my phone number to guys even when I don't care to talk to them again. I hate doing that, but sometimes I can't think of an excuse fast enough, and I think it's too mean to give them the wrong number. So, I just give them my real one and screen my calls until they give up.*
>
> —*Jami, thirty-two, Queens, New York*

A ringing phone can be quite a nuisance when we're trying to avoid the caller. The first time is bad enough, but when the calls start coming regularly, we feel guilty and start blaming the victim: Why is he still calling? Isn't it obvious I'm not interested? He's probably a crazy stalker.

In case you're curious, here's what the guy is probably thinking: We had chemistry. She gave me her number. If I could just get her on the phone, I know she'd be interested. At the very least, I'll be able to figure out why she doesn't want to pursue the connection.

To avoid throwing perfectly innocent men into a frenzy, your best bet is to be straightforward. When a guy you have no intention of seeing again asks for your number, tell him: "I'm sorry. You seem like a great guy. But I don't give out my phone number." If he persists, you can stand up for yourself. After all, why should you be inconvenienced by a stranger's calls if you don't want to be? Here are three ways to beat his objections:

- "I have a boyfriend." If he's smart, he'll assume you're telling the truth and walk away with his ego intact. According to Jewish thought, this kind of lie is preferable to the truth because it is told with the intention of sparing another person's feelings.

- "Sorry, no exceptions. A rule is a rule." This will make you seem so rigid, he'll lose all desire to call you.

- "Like I said, it's been nice talking to you, but I just don't feel the chemistry." What can you do? You can't control how you feel.

Here is what *not* to do:

- *Give out a fake phone number.* Every time you sense the urge to take this coward's way out, take a few moments to perform the following visualization exercise: Picture the guy you're talking to telling his friends about this cute girl who gave him her number. Imagine him waiting the prerequisite twenty-four to seventy-two hours, getting all excited before the big call, maybe even practicing his opening lines. Then, envision him dialing the digits and being greeted with "Hello, and welcome to movie phone." Talk about a tearjerker.

- *Give out your real number and then screen your calls.* The poor guy will never understand why you liked him well enough to give him your number but not enough to pick up the phone. If you want to relate to how some men feel when this happens, you need only think of the last time you went to a party and clicked with a great guy. Maybe you spent half the evening in scintillating conversation, maybe he went out of his way to express his more than carnal interest in you, maybe he even made a big show of asking for your number, and maybe he never called. Why? You'll never know. All you can do is spare others the same aggravation by being honest. If he has your number and isn't shy about using it, Jewish ethics dictate that you not ignore another person's suffering. So, for God's sake, pick up the phone, tell him you're too busy to talk or involved in a whirlwind romance, and put an end to his anguish once and for all.

*I met a very good looking girl in a bar. We talked for about five minutes but then her friends wanted to leave and started pulling her away. I had to ask for her number fast. She gave it to me and when I called we arranged to go out that weekend. After dinner, we decided to go to my friend's party. I was kind of anxious about introducing her so soon, but I figured why not? Well, I'll never make that mistake again. As soon as we got there, her personality went from sixty to zero. I don't know if she was intimidated or if she didn't like my friends or what, but everyone thought she was very rude. She would't talk to anyone. I was turned off completely.*

—Scott, twenty-seven, San Francisco

The Torah commands us to "love the stranger, for you yourselves were strangers in the land of Egypt." (Deuteronomy 10:19) What this means in Scott's case is that he should first look to himself to see if his date had reason to be surly. Did he introduce her around? Did he attempt to facilitate conversation between her and his friends? Did his friends react warmly to the introduction? The responsibility lay with Scott and his friends to make his date feel comfortable because she is the stranger at the party. While "Love the stranger" is a commandment that technically applies to converts from other faiths, its implications revolve mostly around hospitality.

If after careful consideration Scott can honestly say that he and his friends had done all they could to make his date feel welcome and comfortable, then her unresponsiveness may be the result of any number of factors. Maybe she's shy or introverted. Maybe she is self-absorbed or judgmental. Or perhaps something she ate at dinner just didn't agree with her. If Scott is still interested in his date, he may want to try to discern what is at the root of her behavior before forming an opinion and embarking on a course of action. In any case, we can all take a lesson from this particular example: Whether we're meeting our date's friends or our friend's date, we should always strive to put our best foot forward if we wish to avoid any future unpleasantness.

## KEEP FAR AWAY FROM FALSEHOOD

*I was on a first date the other night. We had dinner and when the check came, I reached for my wallet. When he didn't try to stop me, I had to offer to split the bill. And he let me! He said, "Well, if you prefer." Of course, I don't prefer. It was just a polite gesture. He ate twice as much as me! But I couldn't very well say that, now could I? Right now, he's probably wondering why I'm not returning his calls. That's why.*

—Sandy, thirty-four, Phoenix

Jewish ethics has a name for this common dating scenario, it's called "stealing the mind." When we make offers that we anticipate will be refused only to make the other person believe that we are nicer, more generous, or more independent than we really are, we are deceiving them. Maybe Sandy made the effort to be polite or because she wanted to be perceived as a modern woman who can pay her own way. Whatever her intentions, she definitely got what she asked for.

Her date may have thought she was a feminist and taken her

up on the offer out of politeness. Regardless, Sandy's anger is misdirected. If she's going to be angry with anyone, she should be angry at herself for making the offer. Her date had every right to accept, so she cannot use that as an excuse for ignoring his calls.

If you've ever found yourself in a similar situation and experienced the same feelings of frustration and resentment, then it's high time you either reevaluate your feelings or stop offering to pay. Remember, when you put an offer on the table, you have to be prepared to deal with the consequences. If that means avoiding the fallout by not offering to pay until the third, fifth, or eighth date, by all means resist the urge to reach for your credit card in hopes of having him shoo it away. Instead, just say "Thank you for dinner. It was great."

Think of it this way, would you rather have a friend offer to foot the bill for lunch and then complain to everyone what kind of a no-good cheapskate you are for letting her do it, or would you rather she not make the offer and spare you the trouble of having to divine her true intentions?

Obviously, none of this is to say that you should not offer to split the bill with your dates. If you can go dutch without experiencing residual feelings of resentment and anger, more power to you!

> About two weeks after breaking up with my boyfriend, I met another guy. He asked me out and even though I wasn't over my ex, I said yes. He was so into me that I threw myself into the new relationship, hoping I would grow to like him more. Unfortunately, after a few months, I realized it was just a rebound. I wish I had feelings for him, but they just weren't there. I waited a couple of months, and then broke it off. He was really hurt, but what could I do? I tried.
>
> —Sabina, twenty-eight, Boulder, Colorado

There's a non-Jewish saying that goes, "If you can't be with the one you love, love the one you're with." Anyone who has ever had a rebound relationship will understand the meaning of this statement and it's potential pitfalls only too well. When it comes to rebound romance, caution is a must.

To deal fairly with a rebound lover, you first need to understand the workings of your heart. If you are honest with yourself, you'll be able to be straightforward with your new companion. Take the quiz in "Romantic vs. Pragmatic" below to find out what you can expect from your rebound relationship.

When you are truly ready for a commitment, rebound romance can lead to a solid future. If, on the other hand, you are not prepared to open your heart to someone who is looking to take the next step, then you may inadvertently be using your new boyfriend to get over your last one—a major no-no as far as Jewish ethics are concerned.

Since it's difficult to make sense of your feelings at tumultuous times, be as honest as possible with your newfound love interest. Tell him you've just gotten out of a relationship. Tell him you're not sure what you're looking for. Tell him you're not over your ex. As long as you make sure he has all the information he needs to keep his emotions in check and to make a well-educated decision, you'll know you did right by all involved.

## ROMANTIC VS. PRAGMATIC

As SJFs, we fall into two camps: romantic and pragmatic. The former usually cannot love or commit to anyone who does not inspire them with a strong emotion, whereas the latter can summon these feelings and forge a commitment at will. Even if your dream is a husband, two kids, and a house in the burbs, your actions may show that you are more interested in romantic no-tions of love than in the reality of a serious, committed relationship. Here is a simple true/false quiz to give you an idea of where you truly stand.

1. If I don't feel any sparks with a guy right away, I move on.  T  F

2. My friends say I am too picky.  T  F

3. It's a turn-off when a guy calls me every day.  T  F

4. I will not settle down until I meet my soul mate.  T  F

5. The guys I like are usually players.  T  F

6. People think I'm a player.  T  F

7. All the ex-boyfriends I've really cared about have been afraid of commitment.  T  F

8. I want to be sure I marry the right person, so I don't end up trapped in a loveless marriage.  T  F

9. I'm usually the one who ends the relationship.  T  F

10. I fall in and out of love quickly.  T  F

## SCORING AND RESULTS

If you answered true to five or more of the statements, you are a romantic and may have a fear of commitment. Even if you're tired of the dating game and would like nothing better than to quit playing the field, your propensity to stress romance over practical matters may mean that stability, security, and predictability are not high atop your list of priorities.

There's nothing wrong with being romantic, but this character trait can have dire consequences for rebound relationships. If you get involved while you're feeling vulnerable, you may try to transfer your affections from your ex to the rebound and overlook major incompatibilities in the process. Then, when the dust settles and you're your old self again, you'll realize that this is not the perfect match you've been holding out for and that you are far too commitment shy to accept a guy simply because he's ready, willing, and able.

For those of you who are not as fearful of the "c-word," a rebound can blossom into a substantial relationship. The more time you spend with a person, the more attached you may become. If the new guy provides you with the stability that was missing in your last relationship, you are likely to develop strong feelings with time.

> *Being single in New York, I meet a lot of men. I can usually tell if I'm interested by the end of the first date. Sometimes, I know there's no future, but if he's generous and takes me out to a great dinner or a concert, I will continue to see him anyway. I like the good life. What's wrong with that?*
>
> *—Arianne, twenty-eight, New York*

Using another person as a meal/concert ticket is strictly verboten where Jewish ethics are concerned. If you are more interested in your date's investment portfolio than in who he is as a person, the right thing to do is to stop seeing him all together.

Be honest with yourself. It's one thing to be attracted to a man who just happens to be wealthy and quite another to date a man simply because you want to upgrade your lifestyle with great restaurants, the theater, and all-expense-paid vacations. Jewish thought considers people who date for money alone to be superficial, materialistic, and generally in possession of bad character.

Leading a person to believe that you care about him when you care only about his wallet also happens to be dishonest. Just consider how you would feel if you realized that the man you were dating was with you only because of your looks. How would you feel if you learned that he didn't want to know anything more about you? That he viewed you as little more than a pretty accessory to show off to his friends?

If you had any genuine feelings for your boyfriend, this kind of realization would be devastating—if not, then according to Jewish ethics, you shouldn't have been with him to begin with.

## SPEAKING OUT: WHEN TO BE A CRITIC

*I'd been dating Dan for a couple of months. He had this bad habit of making plans and then forgetting about them. He'd call the day we were supposed to go out together and say, "So, what are you up to tonight?" This was so aggravating, I finally had to break up with him because I was sick of being angry all the time.*

—Natalie, twenty-two, Portland, Oregon

While some may say that Natalie was right to break up with Dan because of his unreliable ways, the truth is not so cut and dried. Had Natalie warned Dan about how his flaky ways made her feel and found that there was no improvement, the split would have been well warranted. However, in this case, Natalie never expressed her anger to Dan until it had built up to unmanageable proportions and she had to break off the relationship.

According to Jewish thought, we have a responsibility to tell our friends and significant others when they are doing something wrong. Especially if their mistakes are likely to have dire consequences—such as the loss of a relationship. If we do not reprove the people in our lives, we are contributing to their failure. In other words, if you're not part of the solution, you're part of the problem.

Constructive criticism is one of the biggest benefits we can derive from our friends. Natalie had a responsibility to express her misgivings to Dan. Had she held Dan accountable for his actions, he could have learned a valuable lesson and cleaned up his act. While Dan certainly shares in the blame, Natalie also deserves credit for ruining what may very well have been a good relationship.

*My ex-boyfriend drove me crazy. He had terrible manners, his sense of humor was asinine and he never had anything insightful to add to any conversation. I'd always tell him that he was acting obnoxious, but it was no use. We just weren't compatible.*

—*Samantha, twenty-nine, Palo Alto, California*

The difference between constructive and destructive criticism is simple. Constructive criticism focuses on shortcomings that a person can change and is phrased in a way that would encourage him to make the requisite changes, but destructive criticism revolves around flaws that cannot be improved and is presented in the form of insults.

There is little that Samantha's boyfriend could do about his mental capacity or maturity level. Criticizing him for not being smart enough is hurtful . . . not to mention about as effective as someone constantly pointing out that you are not tall enough or old enough. It's a fact of life. Either accept it or tell your partner that you're incompatible and move on—just don't stick around to make his life miserable for lack of anything, or anyone, better to do.

## THE GOLDEN RULES OF BREAKUPS

*My boyfriend of one year has been being very inconsiderate lately. He no longer calls me every day, we've been hanging out less, and he's often in a bad mood when we're together. I love him so much, I just want it to be the way it was in the beginning. I'm afraid he's going to leave me. So I've just been acting extra nice to him and trying to avoid confrontation. I don't know what else to do.*

—*Lara, thirty-seven, Austin, Texas*

Applying Hillel's Golden Rule can be especially difficult where matters of the heart are concerned. Certainly, there is no single right way to handle a problem like Lara's, but her "turn the other cheek" approach will not help matters. It's a simple matter of self-defense and responsible behavior. If you care about yourself at all, you will not allow someone to hurt you over and over again without a confrontation. As Hillel said, "If I am not for myself, who will be for me?"

If you are ever in a situation where you feel that someone who once cared for you is pulling away, resist the natural impulse to give chase. Look back to a time when you were the one who lost interest in a relationship. Remember the deep freeze that fell over your heart and how it manifested itself in your actions toward the former object of your affection. Consider what you wanted at the time. Distance, time, and space to breathe, to think, to make a decision. If your partner did not sense your reticence, he probably stepped up his efforts to win you over like Lara is doing. Being extra nice, extra affectionate . . . extra annoying, given that all you really wanted was to be alone.

Spare yourself the pain of repeated rejection. When your instincts tell you that your significant other is losing interest, stand up for your right to be respected and appreciated by pulling back as well. Don't call, don't go out of your way to be nice, nix the displays of affection. If he doesn't revert back to his former loving self within a week's time, confront him. Bring the issue into the open, tell him what's been bothering you, and try to get him to open up about his feelings. Maybe even suggest a trial separation. If he takes the bait, you'll know he was trying to get out of the relationship. If he insists that you can work it out, follow your heart and see if his behavior improves.

*I just got back on the dating scene after a four-year relationship and quickly realized that the more things change the more they stay the same. I'm still really bad about telling people that I don't want to see them again. In the few months since I started dating, I've probably blown-off about five guys. A friend of mine says I owe these guys an explanation, but I don't think I owe them anything after three or four dates. I'd much rather a guy just phased me out than sat me down for a heart-to-heart about how he doesn't see our so-called relationship going any-where. How awkward!*

—Allison, thirty-one, Grosse Point, Michigan

No one likes to be the bearer of bad news. Sadly, there is no formula for the proper way to abort a relationship still in its fetal stages. Most of the time, four dates do not a relationship make so we should be able to cut things off with a polite excuse, an offer of friendship, or even an unreturned phone call or two.

If the phone calls persist, however, a short conversation is in order. Messages such as "I'd really appreciate it if you called me back, just to let me know that you're still among the living" need to be returned. Even when you don't feel the need to explain, if your onetime friend is desperate for an explanation or just some form of closure, by all means, oblige.

For the more impetuous among us, four dates could signify a serious emotional investment. If you've had a few very intense dates and you feel that your companion has grown seriously attached whereas you've had occasion to reconsider, do not behave as if all you had were four casual dates. Don't even try to weasel out of your responsibility to formally end the relationship by avoiding his calls. Instead, pick up the phone and kindly express that you are not prepared to embark upon a relationship. As bad as you feel while you're on the phone, you'll feel that much better for having done the right thing when the deed is done.

*When my ex told me that he didn't think we were compatible, he asked if we could be friends. After the shock wore off, I agreed. Unfortunately, our friendship is really just an intimate relationship without commitment or exclusivity. Friends with benefits. This would be a dream come true, except for the fact that I'm completely in love with him. Sometimes, I want to break it off, but then I think, isn't it better to have a little of something good than nothing at all?*

—Ava, twenty-five, San Francisco

Not to take anything away from Ava's problem, but this is such a common scenario that other people's experiences may shed light on the best way to handle this complicated situation. Nine out of ten times, it ends the same way . . . it's called the long and painful good-bye.

The chances for a happy ending are almost zilch when two people want different things from their relationship. In this case, it's Ava's needs that are not being met. By staying with her "friend," she thinks that she will wear him down with her persistence, melt his reserve, or become indispensable over time. Unfortunately, he will never have any incentive to give her what she wants because his happiness depends on her dissatisfaction. The conditions that allow him to continue the relationship are the very ones that are making Ava miserable. Worse still, this type of an arrangement requires Ava to lie to herself. To maintain the relationship, she needs to tell herself that she is satisfied with the way things are when she clearly and obviously wants so much more.

Consider what you would want a guy to do if you didn't want anything more than a no-strings-attached relationship but he was in love with you? Would you want him to hide his feelings and suffer in silence just so you didn't have to feel lonely?

Probably not. At least not if you cared about him and didn't want to see him get hurt.

Ava cannot change the way she feels any more than her boyfriend can change his feelings. It's a sad fact of life that our emotions exist independently of our reason. We cannot make ourselves fall in and out of love with someone. What we can do is use our minds to figure out when a relationship is not healthy because it makes us feel bad. You know what you want. If you're not getting it, don't invest any more time and energy. Instead, cut your losses, because the more you sacrifice your own needs and wishes to maintain a relationship, the more invested you will become. Meanwhile, the person for whom you are playing the martyr will not have cause to follow suit. In the end, you'll only be more dependent on him, while his feelings for you will not change.

## THE LAST WORD

The key to being a nice Jewish girl is to be nice to yourself first. There is simply no other way to understand Hillel's advice to not do unto others as you would not have done unto you. After all, if you treat yourself poorly, why should you treat others any better? If you don't love yourself, how can you truly love anyone else? And, if you don't understand the machinations of your own heart, how can you relate to anyone else's? Since being an ethical dater is all about understanding other people's feelings and doing what you can to avoid hurting them, you have to make sense of your own emotions first. The process can take a lifetime—especially because in our action- and results-oriented society, merely facing and admitting to our feelings can require a great effort.

## THOU SHALTS AND THOU SHALT NOTS

For your regular, run-of-the-mill breakup (definition: one that's brought about by a loss of affection rather than infidelity or verbal or physical abuse), sensitivity is of paramount importance. How will you explain your change of heart to your boyfriend when you can't point to any obvious mistreatment on his part?

**NOT LIKE THIS:**

- "It's not you, it's me." Everyone knows and hates this cliché.

- "Maybe later, when I'm not such a mess." What if later never comes? Make sure the dumpee isn't sitting around waiting for you to see the light.

- "I'm leaving you for Mr. Right." If you have met someone you prefer to your boyfriend, for God's sake, keep it quiet. No one wants to hear that the current love of their life found a better man.

- "You're too _____. You're not _____ enough." Resist the temptation to criticize your soon-to-be ex, even if he pummels you with questions like: "What's wrong?" "Why?" "What about me didn't you like?" The truth is that if you'd been ready for a relationship, in love with him, or simply more compatible, it would not have mattered that he was too talkative or not ambitious enough. So don't rationalize your lack of emotion and make your ex feel that his human imperfections were what sent you packing.

- "What do you say? One last time? For old times' sake?" Unless you want to rob him of every possible ounce of satisfaction, have the courtesy to let him bring it up.

**BUT LIKE *THIS*:**

● "You're an amazing person, we're just not right together." Sometimes, two people just aren't meant to be a couple. You'll be letting him know that it's no one's fault. It won't make him feel better, but it won't make him feel worse.

● "I am not emotionally ready for a relationship." This says "it's not you, it's me" without adding insult to injury.

● "It's not working. I am not happy." Simple, honest, and to the point.

● "I just don't feel it. I wish I could be with you, but I can't control my heart." This sends the message that there is nothing wrong with him, but as great as he is, you are not in control of your feelings.

● "I'll miss you." He will certainly be missing you. Even if you know full well that all you will feel is relief, there's no harm in letting him think you'll share his pain.

While you work to become the kindest and most compassionate person you can be, you can learn from the experiences and advice of people who have been in similar circumstances. That's why this chapter covered basic dating scenarios—some fairly straightforward, others more complicated. I hope this advice provided some insight and assistance. Of course, this is only the tip of the iceberg. If you're interested in learning more about how to apply Jewish ethics to your life, Additional Resources on page 179 provides suggested reading material.

# chapter five

## Sex and the Jewish Girl

*I've had all kinds of experiences. From monogamy to casual encounters. I went through a long phase where sex was just that and nothing more. But I never felt satisfied. I'm now becoming more aware of my emotional needs and changing some of my sexual habits. I won't sleep with anyone just because I find him attractive. Which means no more sex after one too many margaritas, no more sex on the first date, and no more sex when I'm not feeling something more than just physical for the person.*

*I've been channeling my excess sexual energy into creative and intellectual pursuits like making jewelry and studying gemology so I don't feel as tempted to throw caution to the wind and do something that I may later regret. I don't know what any of this has to do with being Jewish. It's just a system that works for me.*

—Jennifer, thirty, Portland, Oregon

Sex and Judaism . . . what does the one have to do with the other? One is a primal act, as basic to the survival of the species as eating and drinking. The other is the world's first monotheistic religion as well as a system of values and ethics that can be used to guide every aspect of one's life, including sex.

Forget what you've heard about doing it through a hole in a bedsheet, that's not what kosher sex is all about. From the Torah to the Talmud to the Kabbalah, Judaism has always had a great deal to say on the subject of sexuality. But for most of us SJFs, the strict rules of religion seem to have lost their relevance. The world has changed since the days when Deuteronomy decreed "that there shall be no intercourse with a woman, without previous marriage."

The ban on premarital sex was borne of a time when Bar Mitzvahs turned boys into men. Literally. And marriage, usually arranged by the parents, occurred not long thereafter. (The Talmud sanctions marriage as early as thirteen for boys and twelve for girls.) Back then premarital sex meant doing it as a teen, long before one was considered emotionally ready.

Today, teenage sex is still frowned upon, but many of us have cast aside religious doctrines written centuries before like so many articles of children's clothing. They no longer fit. They're useless. Outdated. Hopelessly beyond the point. There's just one catch: Unlike our outgrown children's clothes, which are replaced by larger, more age-appropriate models, the rules of religion have no sequel, no new and improved edition.

For lack of better options, we built our ideas of sexual propriety around religious dictates until the late 1960s. Back then, everyone knew that good girls don't and good Jewish girls *definitely* don't. But the 1970s took care of all that. Or so some thought. Billed as a return to a state of grace—in which sex is natural, free of the stigma of original sin—the sexual revolution instead perverted the concept of free love. Love and sex became one and the same. Hey, girls, go have sex with someone. Anyone. That's what spreading the love is all about.

When the sexual revolution backfired into a full-scale battle of the sexes, many realized that without a system to guide and support us, we tend to make up the rules as we go along. No wonder there is so much confusion in the realm of our sex lives. Sure, we have a surplus of psychotherapists and self-help books to assist us. There are also a number of spiritual and philosophical works one can read to gain some wisdom and perspective. Many of these sources, however, just adapt what rabbinic scholars like Moses Maimonides, author of the *Mishneh Torah,* have been saying for centuries: Find the golden mean (*shvil hazahav*), your balance between hedonism and asceticism, self-indulgence and self-denial.

As an SJF, I wondered why many of us spend so much time reading books by everyone from Dr. Brothers to Dr. Phil, and so little time thinking about how we can reinterpret Jewish laws so that they apply to our lives. While many of the dictums may be far out and biased against women, even the most old-fashioned can be deconstructed to reveal great meaning and universal truths.

Since a moment of insight is worth a lifetime of experience, the goal of this chapter is to find new meaning in old scripture. Once we probe beneath the surface—that is to say, beyond the literal translation—of the many laws and dictums, we find that Judaism's take on sexuality has a great deal to offer those of us interested in more fulfilling sex lives. This chapter will explore the many ways you can establish a connection between your life and Judaic principles to:

- Infuse meaning and spirituality into your sex life.

- Make your every sexual experience more pleasurable and emotionally satisfying.

- Figure out when it's time to boost or reduce your sex drive.

- Set yourself free from feelings of guilt and regret.

- Recognize the difference between destructive and constructive sexual behavior.

## JEWISH SEX 101: THE BASICS

Since traditional Judaism does not condone premarital sex, most of the rules and regulations that govern the expression of sexuality are intended for married couples. However, as birth-control-pill-popping, condom-toting, vibrator-using contemporary SJFs, there is nothing keeping us from using the techniques put forth in the Jewish teachings to reap all the rewards of a deeper, more meaningful sex life. Let's begin with Debra's story:

> I noticed a pattern in my relationships. I would meet someone who I thought was a lot like me, fall head over heels, and get involved in these passionate love affairs within a week's time. Eventually, though, the initial high would subside and I'd realize that I had imagined the whole thing. I hadn't been making love to the men in my bed but to the men I wanted them to be.
>
> —Debra, twenty-five, Brooklyn

Debra's modus operandi brought her nothing but heartache and disappointment—the very same feelings that Jewish teachings want to help us avoid. What Debra describes is a state of selfishness, when sex is just about one person: Me. My wants, my needs, my perspective, my vivid imagination. Worse still, as Debra has recognized, it's a self-absorption that is ultimately self-destructive in that it demands immediate gratification irrespective of the emotional consequences. What Judaism espouses is quite different. Jewish teaching dictates the following.

## SEX IS THE UNION OF MAN, WOMAN, AND GOD

The simple idea that "sex is the union of man, woman, and God" is how Jewish tradition defines good sex. To figure out how this applies to our personal lives, we need to consider the meaning of the words *union* and *God*.

Whether or not we believe in God, we can all relate to the idea of a God. Like the Jewish God, we are alone in the universe. Similar as we are, we're also extremely different. Each of us sees things our own way. Like God, we cannot control other people because the one thing neither human beings nor God can rule is free will. So, even though we can never attain God's immortality, we all have God's potential within us.

If we see God as the Creator, then one way to interpret this phrase is that we unite with God when we too become creators. To make sex a true union of man, woman, and God, we create a new world custom-made for ourselves and our partners, a world in which there is mutual understanding and acceptance of differences, where we know each other and are comfortable together without trying to control or inhibit each other's free will. Sex consummates this creation, allowing us to know each other completely and be comfortable with each other in our most vulnerable, naked state.

For the ultimate sexual experience, we have to forge this union of souls. It's not always easy, especially when chemistry is strong and hormones are raging. As Debra described at the start of this section, the temptation to jump in headlong can be overwhelming—particularly when we feel as if we've known someone our whole lives after just a few days.

Fortunately, Judaism has always been forgiving when it

comes to lapses in judgment . . . especially where sex is concerned. Our religion does not condemn imperfection so much as it encourages us to strive for the ideal. Yielding to desire is understandable, just as long as we don't indulge ourselves too long in this "fall from grace." For help on calming down a whirlwind romance, regaining perspective, and getting back on the road to creating a real, lasting union, check out the "To Know . . . in the Biblical Sense" on page 107.

> *Sex? Hmmm . . . I think it's been about a year since I've had any. It's driving me nuts, but what can I do? I'm in medical school. It's all I can do just to pass my exams. I don't have time to get dressed up and go guy hunting. I live in Miami and I know there are tons of opportunities, but even if I met someone now, I wouldn't be able to give him any attention. I'm so busy.*
>
> —Amaya, twenty-six, Miami

Amaya has some good points. She knows that at this time, she cannot sustain both a personal life and a passing grade point average. In the old days, when women had nothing but personal lives, religious mandates dictating the necessity of keeping a balance between business and pleasure were directed solely at men.

## SEX IS THE DUTY OF THE SJM AND THE RIGHT OF THE SJF

A husband owes his wife three things: food, clothing, and sexual pleasure (or *onah*). Substitute "woman" for *wife,* "man" for *husband,* and now you're talking the SJF's language: dinners, shopping sprees, and sexual gratification. What more can a girl want?

The truth is that, nowadays, most of us can afford our own dinners (thank you very much). And all we need for a good shopping spree are some willing girlfriends. But sexual gratification

# TO KNOW . . . IN THE BIBLICAL SENSE

The Torah refers to the sexual act as "to know." Since whirlwind romance can send mutual knowledge and understanding flying out the nearest window, it's important to regain our footing when we feel that head-over-heels sensation.

As much fun as it is to feel vital and alive, these emotions don't last forever. More important, the highs are often followed by equally intense lows. Judaism warns against such extremes. And not for nothing. Creating a stable connection between the hearts, minds, and spirits of two separate entities who just happen to have compatible pheromones takes work and concentrated effort.

The following connection–correction process will either strengthen a viable union or help dissolve one that is untenable. Use it whenever you feel the rush of sexual attraction going to your head.

• **Express yourself:** As the world's most famous kabbalist, Madonna, once said, "Express what you've got." Through word or deed, let your paramour know where you stand. Be open, honest, and forthcoming with your opinions. Judaism gives no props to withholders. If you don't want to share your inner self with your partner, the sex is going to suffer. Consider waiting to have sex until you are no longer afraid to reveal your true self.

• **Pay attention:** Watch for your partner's reactions. Small signs like facial expressions, off-hand comments, and casual touches carry a lot of weight. So do your feelings, as they may be a reaction to those of your partner. It's a fine balance. You don't want to gloss over any negative signs just because they don't fit in with what you want and are painful to acknowledge, but neither do you want to give positive signals undue weight just because they reinforce your wishes.

- **Seek answers:** To deepen your connection, ask questions. "What do you mean?" is a great one and is surprisingly a lot less popular than we think. Communication is flawed. People say something, and we presume to understand. But every experience is different, so try not to foist your own ideas onto your consort. Instead, ask him to explain the thought process behind his statements. If you encounter resistance, it just may be too soon for sex.

- **Relate:** To step out of your own little world and create a new one with your partner you need to stand in his shoes. If after doing this, you still find that his behavior seems random and unreasonable, it may be that you are putting yourself in his situation and forgetting that he is a different person. Maybe you would do things differently, but then again, you *are* different. Accept these differences because you have no choice. Then make your decision: Will you invest yourself deeper in the relationship or are you two simply too different to make it work?

remains a deal breaker. The rule of *onah* was set up during the days when men worked and women took care of the household. The idea was that nothing, not even a job, should detract from family life.

The Talmud actually decrees how many times a week a man is required to have sex with his wife. The quality and quantity varies according to the occupation: "Men of independent means—every day, workmen—twice a week, ass drivers—once a week, camel drivers—once a month, and sailors—at least once every six months." (*Ketubot* 5:6). A man must bring his partner to orgasm, or he has failed to fulfill his obligation. Furthermore, if he cannot perform his duties as often as required due to professional stress and obligations, he must find a new livelihood.

The law provides some food for thought. In today's relationships, the rules are different. Just as men and women share the burden of paying for food and clothing, the responsibility for initiating sex has also become a two-way street. Whereas women were once presumed to be the shy gender and the onus was on men to play the aggressor we are now equals capable of understanding that there are just as many shy men walking the earth as there are shy women.

So much has changed, but the crucial function that sex serves within our lives and relationships remains the same. Lovemaking consummates the attraction that brings people together and strengthens the bonds that keep them there. If we are to extract the same lessons from Hebrew wisdom as do men, we cannot allow our work-related pressures and responsibilities to overshadow ourselves and our personal lives.

## IT IS NOT GOOD FOR AN SJF TO BE ALONE

> *I am Modern Orthodox. I keep kosher. I go to shul every Friday night and Saturday morning. I am* shomer Shabbat, *which means that I don't drive, watch TV, or work on Saturdays. The only allowance I make is sex. I've been living with my boyfriend for two years. He's also Modern Orthodox. I know some people might consider us hypocrites, but we're just not ready to get married yet.*
>
> —Susan, twenty-seven, Palo Alto, California

After all this time, Susan still isn't sure if marriage is for her. However, she is certain that she loves her boyfriend.

The Old Testament dictum that "it is not good for man to be alone" combined with "man shall leave his mother and father and cleave to his wife" has traditionally been taken to mean that we should all marry. When considered along with the Torah's first mitzvah, to "be fruitful and multiply," it's clear that we are also compelled to procreate. All told, the Orthodox view is that the purpose of sex is to have children and companionship.

However, if a couple is unable to bear children, they are still encouraged to have sex on a regular basis for the purposes of companionship, pleasure, and spiritual expression. Celibacy is simply not an option in Judaism, as it is in Catholicism. We have no priests and nuns. No one is "married to God" and everyone is encouraged to enjoy sex.

By commanding people to marry before having sex, talmudic scholars were acknowledging the social and emotional consequences of abortive sexual relationships (crimes of passion caused by jealous rage, illegitimate children, shame upon the family, decreased marriage prospects, etc.). Today, most of us would sooner risk the possibility of hurt feelings than marry someone before we've seen what they're like in bed. Furthermore, many of us are spiritually and emotionally ready to have sex but not prepared to get married. So we reinterpret the laws and seek new meaning in old wisdom.

We grow as people through a series of emotionally and physically intimate encounters. Through our relationships, we learn about ourselves, how we are alone and how we react to others. In the end, heartbreak can be a wonderful thing all in itself, making us wiser, more compassionate, and better prepared for real commitment. In the end, if we take the time to understand and learn from our past mistakes, come to the conclusion that our lives are not all or nothing propositions, and strive to be as responsible and respectful as possible, we are in keeping with the meaning of the Torah, if not with its language.

## THE BUSINESS OF PLEASURE

*I've got no problem with one-night stands or casual sex. I am a very sensual and sexual person. When I want sex and don't get it, trust me, you don't want to be around me. I know these things about myself, so I always set the ground rules. First of all, condoms are a must. And if it's just sex, I make it clear that I'm not interested in a relationship beforehand so that I can fully enjoy the sex without feeling that I'm somehow lying to get the guy into bed. Obviously, if I like the guy, I'll wait longer so I can get to know him better and get some sense of whether he returns my feelings. I'm not looking to get my heart broken here.*

—*Candice, twenty-seven, Atlanta, Georgia*

Candice is an attorney, not a sex maniac. She works more than fifty hours a week and goes out only four to six times a month. She is looking for a deeper connection, but cannot tolerate long bouts of abstinence. Like many of the women I interviewed, she is an expert at separating lust from love and does not need to deny her physical appetites to keep her emotions under control.

Jewish tradition has it that "in the world to come a man will have to face judgment for every legitimate pleasure which he denied himself." If we think of legitimate pleasure as anything that gives us joy without hurting either ourselves or others, then Candice certainly has the right idea (especially since she follows the Rabbinic teaching that sexual activity based on lies is destructive). Whether or not we believe in an afterlife or "the world to come," we can all look to people who live to regret foregoing pleasure and not living their lives to the fullest.

For many of us, casual sex is simply not pleasurable. We either feel self-conscious, uncomfortable, and unable to achieve orgasm or we are not stimulated by the idea of having sex with someone whom we don't know very well or like all that much. Whatever our reasons for not enjoying one-night stands, Jewish tradition holds that we'd be smart to recognize our feelings and act accordingly by holding out for a suitable companion.

Then again, for those of us who are of a sensual bent, who feel their spirits flagging and their energy fluctuating simply for lack of sexual gratification, safe, mutually satisfying sex can do far more good than harm. In fact, according to Britain's chief rabbi, Dr. Jonathan Sacks, "The gifts of God are to be found in this world as well as the next, and the ability to enjoy is itself a religious experience."

In the end, there is a world of difference between a person who engages in weekly orgies and one-night stands, thinking of little other than sex eighteen hours a day, and going to bed with one person after another in a misguided attempt to find love or escape reality and a person who takes the time to understand her physical, emotional, and spiritual needs, then fulfills them as she deems fit. The idea of moderation . . . one of Judaism's greatest gifts to mankind.

## RETURN TO MODESTY

*I used to wear miniskirts to shul, go out to parties and clubs in tight jeans, prance around in bikinis on vacation. But then, my head turned toward ha-Shem. Now, I study the Torah, go to classes every day, and live as a Shomerette.*

*Religion doesn't make life more restrictive, it never makes me feel as if I were missing out on the fun. It makes me feel lucky. It makes me want to tell everyone the treasure I've discovered. It makes me want to climb up onto the roof and shout*

# LETHAL SEX

Sex has been around far longer than Judaism. In fact, Judaism was established in reaction to the pagan "if it feels good, do it" philosophy. Because, lets face it, if immediate gratification were really the be-all-end-all, we'd have no indoor plumbing. Yes, in the name of family, society, and civilization as we know it, a balance had to be struck and the Jews did just that with the Torah.

Defining destructive sexual acts was one of the Torah's major aims. Here are the three most egregious sexual offenses, all punishable by death and in no specific order:

● **Rape:** The Jews' insistence on controlling the potentially destructive forces of anger and sexuality, in other words rape and other forms of violence, was borne of a desire to promote a safe, well-functioning society. Deuteronomy declared rape a capital offense, saying: "if a man comes upon an engaged girl in the open country, and the man lies with her by force, only the man who lay with her shall die. But you shall do nothing to the young girl."

● **Incest:** Nowadays, incest and rape are obviously off limits. But this wasn't always the case. When these ideas were first presented, the Jews were pooh-poohed for their overdeveloped sense of modesty and propriety. Today, these laws are taken as self-evident. Leviticus commands that "None of you shall come near anyone of his own flesh to uncover nakedness; I am the Lord."

Since incest poses a grave danger to family, one of the cornerstones of Judaic tradition, there are nineteen laws forbidding different kinds of incest in the Bible. The list of taboo partners begins with one's father and goes all the way down, through the numerous variations on the incest theme, to a wife's granddaughter and a wife's sister. Although the laws are mainly directed at men (it is forbidden for a man to have relations with his daughter, his sister, his half-sister, and so forth), the idea was that if men are aware of the laws they will not allow women to break them.

● **Adultery:** Today, 70 percent of men cheat on their wives, and women aren't too far behind. Yet when it comes to destructive sexual behavior, Jewish law places adultery right up there with capital offenses such as rape and incest. Thou shalt not so much as covet your neighbor's wife, much less commit actual adultery. It's all right there in the Ten Commandments.

Judaism recognizes adultery as a grave deterrent to family life—to say nothing of the male ego. According to old interpretations, the Torah is really concerned with a married woman having affairs (there's absolutely no mention of coveting your neighbor's husband). Married men can have mistresses, go to prostitutes, and engage in any number of affairs, as long as these are with single women. The sexism hasn't gone unnoticed. The current Jewish position is that male or female, adultery is not kosher.

*to everyone that there's a way to be guaranteed happiness always—it's the only way to be truly happy.*

—*Victoria, twenty-four, Long Island, New York*

Victoria wrote in because she didn't want to see a Jewish girl's book about sex and dating ignore the "Shomerette" perspective— namely that dating and sex don't mix. She found meaning and purpose by accepting God into her heart and became a devout, strictly observant Jew. Judging by her touching essay, veering away from the materialistic toward the spiritual made Victoria a much happier person. Her newfound appreciation for religion gave her the kind of deep fulfillment she had never found when she was looking to the outside world for affirmation.

Wearing longer skirts (instead of micro-minis and jeans), going without makeup, and eschewing the party circuit were just a few of the changes Victoria made to adhere to the pious lifestyle, but they relate directly to the Jewish ideal of sexual modesty. While we modern-day SJFs don't necessarily need to go to such extremes if they don't fit in with our belief system, the emphasis that Judaism places on modesty in our dress can carry as much or as little significance as we choose to attribute to it.

Whether we dress provocatively to engage male attention or simply to show off the fruits of our labor at the gym, the results are often the same: Our focus shifts away from our hearts and minds and onto our bodies. The flaunt-it-if-you've-got-it attitude so encouraged in our society runs counter to Judaic values, which stress inner beauty and self-confidence over the arrogance and self-conceit that are the inevitable results of concentrating too much on appearances.

Nice as it feels to get attention and admiration, being noticed for how we look can lead us to forget that there is more to us than the physical, that we are human beings, full of dignity and potential, and not just sex objects to be gawked at by the opposite sex. Beauty fades. Our true value lies in our kindness, compassion, intelligence, sense of humor, warmth . . . the list goes on and on. Unfortunately, those who place undue importance on the outside often fail to acknowledge, appreciate, and develop their many inner attributes. Flaws in character can also go unnoticed and unresolved. By promoting sexual modesty, Judaism empowers women to focus on the inside and strive for personal strength despite society's negative messages.

Many of the Jewish women I spoke with explained that

although they wear revealing clothing when they go out to clubs, they don't appreciate being leered at by randoms and lechers. The logic is counterintuitive. As a male friend of mine put it, "if you don't want to be chased by dogs, don't rub meat all over your body." Like it or not, showing skin is a mating call. When guys see flesh, their brains tell them we're open for sexual advances (as, sometimes, we are). While this is no excuse for rape and harassment, the warning against women dressing provocatively has been implied ever since the Torah told us about Dinah, sister of Joseph (of *Technicolor Dreamcoat* renown), and her misadventures when she "went out among the daughters of the land." (Genesis 35:1–8)

To put the biblical tale into perspective, Dinah left home and forsook her family's values to barhop with non-Jewish girls and wear the scanty dresses that were all the rage. Dinah ends up sleeping with a man out of wedlock, and her brothers avenge their family's honor by branding her lover a rapist, then killing him and his entire village. Moral of the story: Party girls, beware.

So what's a gal who likes to paint the town to do? Give up our short skirts, tight shirts, and start spending every night in Torah study? What about fun? Good times? These questions bring us right back to where we started, Maimonides' golden mean: All things in moderation and moderation in all things. The following are two ways you can incorporate sexual modesty into your life without destroying your social calendar:

- *Suit yourself:* Clothes can be an attempt to attract attention or an expression of personal style. A way to disguise our inner selves or a means of showing the world who we really are. While the former is superficial and appearance oriented, possibly motivated by some personal insecurities, the latter is grounded in self-confidence and self-awareness. As photographer Annie Liebovitz once said, "Style is substance made visible." Look through your own party clothes.

What do they say about you? If you need help figuring out what type of message your clothes are sending to yourself and to the world, check out the quiz in "Clothes Make the Woman" below.

• *Mind over matter:* The bar scene can bring out the worst in people. So if you're trying to stay true to yourself, you may choose to avoid it entirely for a couple of months. Use the time to pursue your interests. Take the money you would have spent and invest it in some classes. Meet new people in an environment that's caught up in mental rather than physical attributes. Or restrict your socializing to parties and dinners with friends. When you start going to bars and clubs again, you'll probably find that you no longer want to make them your main social outlet.

## CLOTHES MAKE THE WOMAN

Coco Chanel once summed up exactly what's wrong with the fashion industry by saying, "I dress courtesans like chambermaids, and chambermaids like courtesans." What's so wrong with embracing who you are? For her part, Ms. Chanel never dressed like anyone other than herself. What about you? Take the following true/false quiz to find out if your wardrobe can use a little more personal flair.

1. I can go anywhere in my jeans and sneakers, even a nightclub.

2. I wouldn't be caught dead without my high heels.

3. When I go out, I dress to impress regardless of my mood or the occasion.

4. If you want to see skimpy, check out my closet. Christina Aguilera can take a page from my book.

5. When I look good, I feel good.

6. My evening clothes are 180 degrees different than my day clothes.

7. My sexiest clothes are more formfitting than revealing.

8. I'm Sporty, Posh, Baby, Ginger, and Scary all rolled up in one. When I'm feeling tough, I dress like a tomboy. When I'm feeling fun and flirty, I wear a skirt or bright colors.

9. I believe in having a few well-made, well-fitted items rather than a lot of cheap, trendy ones.

10. My clothes are way more outrageous than I am.

## SCORING

Give yourself the following points for each answer and then add the points together for a total score.

1. T = 5, F = 0
2. T = 0, F = 5
3. T = 0, F = 5
4. T = 0, F = 5
5. T = 0, F = 5

6. T = 0, F = 5
7. T = 5, F = 0
8. T = 5, F = 0
9. T = 5, F = 0
10. T = 0, F = 5

## RESULTS

● **40–50 = Fashion victor:** Your personality drives your choice of clothing. You don't dress to look like someone you're not or to catch men's attention. You don't have to. You know who you are and your confidence is appealing enough on its own. The only warning is that you may be a bit too comfortable. If you feel like your clothes are too conservative and don't highlight your true nature, consider investing in a few fun, new pieces.

● **25–35 = Fashion vixen:** Be careful, you're toeing a fine line. There's noth-

ing wrong with wanting to get dressed up and have good time once in a while, but you may be using your clothes and physical appearance to present a false front to the world when the real one would do just as well (if not much better). Putting the way others see you before the way you see yourself may actually undermine your self-assurance in the long run.

- **0–20 = Fashion victim:** You want to look good to attract men, but you don't want men who are attracted only to your looks. Unfortunately, this is exactly what tends to happen when we equate sexiness with exhibitionism. There's a reason most guys at strip bars are more interested in the cocktail waitresses than in the dancers: When it comes to clothing, less is not more. The next time you go out on the town, tone it down a few notches and see what kind of reactions you encounter. They just may surprise you.

## NIDDAH BREAK?

*I never have sex during my period. I know a lot of women who don't care, but to me it seems unhygienic. Sometimes, it's really difficult because I've found that most guys want to have sex regardless. But I'm just not comfortable.*

*It's funny: I've found that my little rule often helps me distinguish between guys I like and the guys I just like to have sex with. I've had a few short relationships where the sex was so good, I thought I was in love. Then my period came around and I could barely stand to be around them.*

*—Ellen, twenty-one, Queens, New York*

Even if you're only remotely familiar with Judaic laws, you probably know that tattoos are a no-no, that cremation is your one-way ticket out of the Promised Land, and that you never ever have sex during "that time of the month." While Ellen's reasons for abstaining from sex while she's menstruating have nothing to do with being Jewish, her ideas of cleanliness and good hygiene as well as the indirect benefits she derives from periodic abstinence are bound up in the Jewish laws of *niddah*.

In their never-ending quest to understand and define the differences between males and females, talmudic scholars spent centuries ruminating upon the implications of menstruation and childbirth. One of their more enduring conclusions was that menstruating women are impure. To avoid the taint that a menstruant puts upon anything she touches, the rabbis set up the *niddah* laws, also known as the purity laws. The crux of this legal code as it is observed today is that a woman may not have intercourse during her period (a minimum of five days). But the rabbis didn't stop there: Not only are women considered impure for the duration of menstruation, but for the seven "clean" days thereafter.

In Orthodox homes (because, lets face it, who else systematically shelves their sex life for that long?), *niddah* laws translate into roughly twelve to fourteen days of abstinence every month. Once this time is up, women cannot be considered pure until they have immersed themselves in a *mikveh*, a large tub filled at least in part with "living" water (usually rainwater or seawater). On the last night of the abstinent period, women take a regular bath or shower to ensure that they are completely clean before stepping into the *mikveh*. When they emerge, they are reborn . . . pure as rain.

Whatever the gender biases and misconceptions of the rabbis who first formulated this practice, there is no denying that *niddah* serves many vital, relationship-fortifying purposes. Even unmarried (and non-Jewish) couples have been known to reap tremendous rewards from imposing a time of separation onto their sex lives. For instance: